Thoughts of

Syd Ball

S C Ball, England

Published in England by

S C Ball
2003

Copyright

© Text S Ball 2003
© Book Cover and Illustrations A R Wilson 2003
© Layout A R Wilson 2003

Printed in England by
Stafford Reprographics Ltd
Bailey Street Stafford ST17 4BG

ISBN   0 9545146 0 2

A CIP catalogue for this book is available from the British Library

All rights reserved. No part of this publication may be reproduced or stored or transmitted in any form or by any means, except as permitted by UK copyright laws, without prior permission in writing from the copyright owner(s).

Contents

Preface		4
Acknowledgments		6
Introductory Thoughts		7
Chapter One	Thoughts on Catching a Pony at Grass	10
Chapter Two	Training to Tie Up	16
Chapter Three	The Intractable Horse	24
Chapter Four	Thoughts on Lungeing	28
Chapter Five	Introducing Side Reins	42
Chapter Six	Thoughts on Long Reining	48
Chapter Seven	Thoughts on Schooling Part 1 : The Basic Principles	58
Chapter Eight	Thoughts on Schooling Part 2 : Lateral Movements, Canter Leads, and Particular Problems Illustrated	74
Chapter Nine	Thoughts on Jumping	90
Chapter Ten	Thoughts on Bitting	100
Glossary		104
Bibliography		106
Index		107

Preface

Peter Beckford wrote 'Thoughts on Hunting' and Molly Sivewright wrote 'Thinking Riding'. In calling this book 'Thoughts on Schooling' I hope to pay homage to these two great writers.

Many books are published each year on the subject of schooling, but most begin with the horse saddled and bridled or wearing lungeing tack. No mention is made of the problems trainers and their grooms may experience when catching a youngster and tacking it up for the first time. Occasionally there is a chapter devoted to so-called evasions; these are sometimes referred to as vices or defences. I have tried to write about these evasions as they occur during schooling, and make no apology for repeating from time to time the logic of going back to a basic lesson whenever an evasion is met. This is the indispensable condition of all training.

I was born in 1922 and so was brought up in the era immediately before and during World War 2 when the horse was still intensively used as a means of transport and on the land. In 1761 a volunteer cavalry force called the Yeomanry had been organised for home defence. It merged with the Territorial Army in 1907.

Young farmers and farm workers went annually to summer camp, taking a young horse with them. This was probably the forerunner of the Pony Club Camp. These Yeomanry trainees came back from Camp with the principles of equitation embedded in their minds which they put into practical use on the farm. Thus a plough team was taught to side-step when turning from the headland back into the furrow and the theory of lateral equitation was put into practice. Importance was placed on giving the horse a good mouth and it was understood that this could only be achieved by the horse relaxing its lower jaw.

As horses were both a living and a pleasure to these farm people, the long summer evenings between seed-time and harvest were spent driving young horses about in long reins to get them supple and submissive to the reins. The radio was in its infancy, and where electricity was non-existent reading was not a viable proposition. Therefore the long winter evenings were spent sitting around the fire at home or in the public bar. Here the conversation would often turn to some aspect of horsemanship. Someone would have a problem with a young horse. Another would have experienced the same and overcome it. Therefore it transpired that the principles laid down at those early Yeomanry Camps were passed on by word of mouth.

When the tractor finally ousted the horse from farm work, I acquired a riding horse and found no difficulty in adapting the rudiments of driving to those of riding. At the age of 47 I gained the B.H.S.A.I. Certificate and have instructed privately and at the Pony Club as well as re-schooling many problem horses, thereby acquiring a vast experience during my lifetime.

It is my hope in jotting down these thoughts that it may be that there is one little tip amongst them that will help some trainer to make at least one horse's lot a happier one.

Syd Ball

Acknowledgements

Many people -and horses- have helped in the making of this book, and we'd like to thank them all.

Special thanks are due to Mr and Mrs Pringle, Johanna Pringle, and Mr and Mrs Freer for their help in providing access to the horses below, and also to Johanna Pringle and Joanne Freer for riding for us.

Horses appearing in the book

Ynysacen Llewelyn	Black Welsh Section D stallion
Snowflake	Welsh part-bred mare
Jack	Chestnut thoroughbred gelding
Vindalandi	Thoroughbred mare
Secret Squirrel	Skewbald cob gelding
Sorcerer's Apprentice	Bay show hunter gelding
The Iron Lady	Dapple grey cob
State Occasion	Chestnut show hunter gelding
Missile Mouse	Weatherbys registered bay eventer mare
Rupert	Bay cob gelding
Flicka	Skewbald Romany-type filly
Red Rose Revelation	Bay show hack

Thanks are also due to Dilys Holmes and the staff at Stafford Reprographics for their help in preparing the book for printing, David Wilson for setting up Alison's computer system and for system/software support, and Jonathan Sturgess for backing the project at every stage.

SB and ARW   May 2003

Introductory Thoughts

'Times change; horses do not,' was the reply given by an old and one-time famous show jumper to a teenager. With the ink not quite dry on some recently acquired horsemaster's certificate, she had had the temerity to venture the opinion that the old man's ideas on horsemanship were out of date.

It is generally thought that ever since Xenophon wrote his treatise on horsemanship twenty-three centuries ago the basic principles of schooling horses have remained the same. It is true that paintings and engravings of the period during the Renaissance show long curb bits and equally long spurs, but this seems to have been compensated for by the amount of time spent by these cavaliers in the riding school to enable them to ride with an independent seat holding the reins in one hand and sword or lance in the other.

In turn, future generations of equestrians may well look askance at our modern method of bridling. Fitting our horses with thick snaffles, most of which are jointed and some double jointed, it seems that we are often obliged to fit tight nosebands of the Grakle, Flash or dropped variety in order to obtain sufficient submission. Surely it is splitting hairs to say which bridling arrangements are the most humane. Since all roads lead to Rome, it is up to the trainer to use his own favourite bridle, i.e. that with which he obtains the submissive response to the rein aids. What is more important is that all aids given should obtain a positive response rather than a negative one.

The habituating of the horse to wear saddle and bridle and carry a rider, or to go quietly in harness, is something that should be done efficiently and expeditiously. On the other hand, further schooling for the job required should progress hand in hand with the mental and physical development of the horse and may take eighteen to twenty-four months to confirm.

Of recent years, the American Monty Roberts has demonstrated how to start a horse within half an hour; that is to say, catch, gentle, and have a rider on its back in that time. During the last century there were several so-called horse tamers who also gave demonstrations on conquering difficult or spoilt horses. With persons who use only brute strength to master a horse the leg straps and hobbles used by these gifted horsemen would be like a razor in the hands of a monkey. Whilst a plebeian horse may quickly submit to having its leg strapped up, a hot blooded horse would fight like a demon, doing itself untold injury, perhaps fatal, before it surrendered.

Some of the famous names of that era were Rarey, Sample, Norton-Smith, O'Sullivan (the Whisperer), and Sydney Galvayne. Captain Horace Hayes and Percy Thorne later wrote books on the subject. All of their methods had a certain similarity: the principle of gently restraining the horse over a period of some minutes until it submitted. Surrender was rewarded by tit-bits, relaxing of the restraining aids, or simply scraping off the sweat and stroking the neck or ears.

In those days horses were a means of transport or draught horses working on the land. They were regarded as more or less expendable, as if one got injured during training there was another to take its place. Time was of the essence, so from a commercial point of view the number of horses that were expeditiously trained in this rough-and-ready way far outweighed the few injured or actually killed.

Today, the majority of horses are kept for pleasure, and when an appreciable sum of money has been invested in the purchase of a suitable horse it would be foolish to maim or spoil it for the sake of not giving more time and patience to its training. Nevertheless the methods of restraint and calming practised by those old-time trainers can be modified to conform with the more humanitarian attitudes of the present day. For instance, by holding a foreleg up using the method explained later, forcibly strapping up the limb with its attendant risk of injury becomes superfluous.

It is truly said that, in the absence of a natural disposition for it, calmness is obtained as a result of submission to the aids. A young horse that readily submits to the consistent aids of its trainer is a happy horse. It will stand to the voice command, can be tacked up easily and if during training it gets in a tizzy it can be persuaded to calm down rather than panic.

Too many people think they can solve all training problems with a big stick. They mistakenly assume the horse can understand why it is being punished. For an example, if a young horse instinctively bites at its handler in response to a rough girthing, the person so bitten will often rub the injury for a full minute and then proceed to give him an almighty thrashing. 'That will teach you not to bite me again,' they say. On the contrary, the next time the horse does bite he will immediately fly away in panic, expecting the same punishment he got the previous time.

The more rational approach is firstly not to girth up so roughly, and secondly to keep an eye on the youngster, tapping it gently across the muzzle with the back of the hand at the precise moment it swings its head round to bite. (The back of the hand is flexible, whereas the palm towards the horse would be either too severe on the horse or sprain the handler's wrist.)

Horses in the wild are gregarious creatures and live in herds. There is usually a master stallion, who during the mating season keeps his harem of mares close by and drives off the weaker stallions he has previously fought and conquered. Out of the breeding season the males are content to live and graze in close proximity to each other. At this time the matriarch mare dominates the herd, placing herself between the rest of the herd and any strange horse or human who ventures too near.

It goes without saying that whether the horse be a mare, gelding or entire, the trainer must assert his authority over the horse to ensure it is he, the human, who is boss of the herd.

This does not mean that irrational brutality is the order of the day, but rather that it is merely necessary to stand up to the instinctive threats the horse levels at the trainer. For example, if the horse advances toward the human with ears back and teeth bared, one has only to step to the side and parry the grab with a mild tap on the nose with one's cap or rolled up piece of paper. Stick or whip should never be used for this purpose as it may accidentally catch the eye.

Throughout the following pages the thoughts are based on the premise that the trainer is empathetic rather than sympathetic. In other words, they should try and think like a horse.

Chapter One
Thoughts on Catching a Pony at Grass

With the exceptions of semi-wild ponies in their native habitat, most horses and ponies living out rely on human beings to supplement their diet in the winter time. They will meet their benefactors at the field gate and almost knock them over in their anxiety to get at the hay and concentrates which have been brought them. As the longer evenings come and the spring grass appears, that same pony will be seen careering round the field with the whole family in pursuit.

It is therefore obvious that some thought and time must be given to the schooling of the pony for him to be caught without effort whenever he is required. Nothing is more frustrating than to spend our valuable time in trying to catch a pony and, when at last honour has been satisfied, there is insufficient time left to ride the little terror.

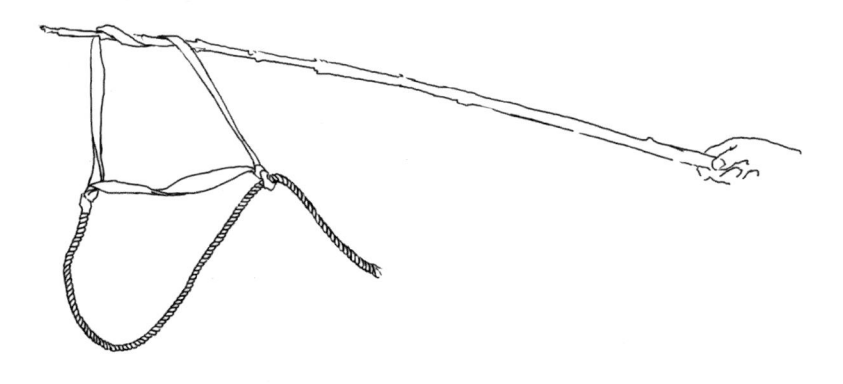

Figure 1 *Halter placed on beanstick*

A few sessions at training the pony to be caught will be time well spent. If a pony is a bad or indifferent jumper, most people will do something about having it schooled; but if it is difficult to catch or load in a horse box, the same people make no effort to school the pony at these things and regularly waste more time with little or no improvement.

Before attempting to catch the pony, we should prepare ourselves with the mental equipment required: empathy, which will be fully explained later on, and the patient determination to carry out, for several sessions if necessary, a preconceived plan of campaign which will, eventually, achieve its object; namely, a pony that can be caught at any time.

The physical equipment should consist of a rope or webbing halter, a fairly long beanstick, and a quantity of wooden fencing with which to fortify one corner of the paddock. A halter should be used in preference to a headcollar, as one can often get a halter on the pony with the help of the beanstick, when one could not get near enough to him to put a headcollar on.

The halter should be fairly new, with no knots or splices in it, and adjusted to approximately the size for the pony. Care must be taken to see that the rope runs freely through the loop on the near side and no knot should be put in it until the pony has been caught. The beanstick should be about six feet in length and preferably of ash. It should be well balanced and trimmed of all shoots in the region where it is held, but left a little bit rougher towards the thin end (as shown in figure 1).

As most fields are not geometrically square, there will be at least one corner which is at an angle of ninety degrees or less. The more acute it is, the better. This corner should be fortified with strong wood, as this is the least likely material to cause the pony injury. Each side of the fence should be fortified for a length of fifteen to twenty feet from the corner. Whilst the pony should never be held in the corner by force, the fence should be built of such height and strength as to deter the pony from either jumping or breaking through it. Needless to say, all barbed wire should be removed from the vicinity.

Empathy is the power of projecting one's personality into (and so fully comprehending) the object of contemplation. We cannot credit ponies with the same reasoning powers that we have ourselves, otherwise they would be our equals, but it would, however, be logical to assume that they connect the winter feeds with little or no handling, and above all, no work; whilst the quickly proffered titbit in spring is quite often followed by an equally quick grab at the mane. If the pony is successfully held, this in turn is followed by energetic work. Since the spring grass is more appetising than the titbit, small wonder that he will not allow himself to be caught.

If the pony can reason that his superior speed can keep him out of reach of one or a number of people, then it is logical to conclude that he should be trained to associate standing still and allowing a halter to be put on his head with pleasant things, whilst running away from humans should be something he associates with unpleasant things.

To this end, the plan of campaign should be to feed the pony titbits as a reward after he has allowed the halter to be put on, and to let a reasonable time elapse between his being caught and actually being worked. This time can be occupied with grooming, picking out feet, and tidying the mane and tail.

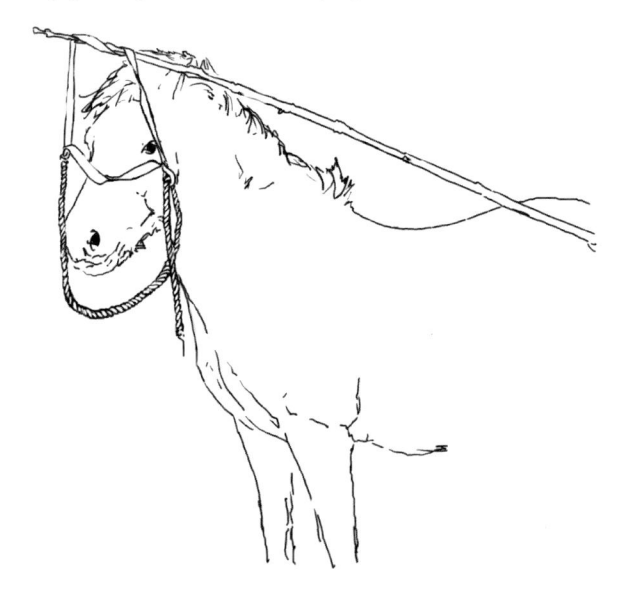

Figure 2a *Putting the halter in place*

If, on the other hand, the pony altogether refuses to be caught, he should be urged to go at the fastest pace he can around the perimeter of the paddock. No attempt should be made to force him into the corner, and the trainer should so manoeuvre himself as to encourage the pony to pass between the himself and the fence by making a supreme effort of speed. In time, and this is where patience and determination are called for, the pony will realise the futility of trying to escape by superior speed and slow down.

By walking parallel with the pony's shoulder, the trainer will eventually be able to persuade the pony to change direction by turning his head away from the trainer and towards the fence. This will be the first step towards training the pony to be driven and the trainer would do well, at this stage, to model his tactics on the manner of a well-trained sheep dog, moving in a wide arc, rather than getting in too close to the pony.

Sooner or later, the pony will come to a halt in the corner that has been prepared and the trainer himself should immediately halt, regardless of how far distant he is from the pony. On no account should he yield to the temptation of moving in close, as the pony must learn that the corner is a place where he can rest. Very steadily, a step at a time, the trainer should move towards the pony, an escape from the corner and a renewal of energetic chasing round the perimeter being preferable to an attempt to hold the pony in the corner by force. This would either result in the pony finding he could break away by superior speed, or, worse still, trying to jump the fence, with drastic consequences.

Figure 2b *Putting the halter in place*

As soon as the trainer can succeed in getting reasonably close to the pony in its corner without it attempting to escape, he should gently stroke the pony with the beanstick, first on the rump and then down the shoulder and underneath the neck. The crown piece of the halter should then be wrapped a couple of times round the thin end of the beanstick, the rough knots that were left on the stick keeping the crown wide apart (figure 1). With the pony standing with his tail in the corner, the beanstick is held in the right hand and the end of the halter rope in the left. Very quietly, the halter is put into place and the stick withdrawn (figure 2a, b). If the pony is quiet, he may now be given a titbit and made much of.

On the other hand, if the pony is wild or nervous, he will shake his head to remove the halter and bolt out of the corner. No harm will have been done, and if the halter rope is of average length he will tread on it from time to time, thus slowing him down and facilitating the process of getting him into the corner once more.

Too long a lead rope is dangerous, as there is not only a risk of the trainer getting his legs tangled up in it, but the pony will take fright at it dragging behind him and, whilst looking back at the trailing rope, will charge headlong through a fence, more often than not causing himself a serious injury.

Figure 3 *The pony coming to meet his trainer in the field*

The secret of success is to have absolute confidence in the method, as the first lesson or two can be very tedious and one is tempted to admit defeat. However, each successive lesson will take less time. Quite soon, the beanstick can be dispensed with and, after stroking the pony with the back of the hand, the halter can be put on easily. It is particularly stressed that the stroking should be done with the back of the hand as, to the pony in a state of apprehension, the touch of the hand palm downwards is very similar to the claw of a predatory beast, from which his instincts will tell him to fly.

By repetition, and in particular through not feeding or caressing him until after he has the halter on his head, the pony will stand or even come to meet the trainer each time he makes his presence known at the paddock gate (figure 3).

Chapter Two
Training to Tie Up

In Western films, horses are tied by the reins to the hitch rail or even 'ground haltered' whilst the goodies and the baddies shoot it out. These horses have been patiently trained over a long period to stand tied up. Occasionally, inexperienced people tie up a horse that has had no previous training. The consequences are often disastrous, as the horse will inevitably struggle to get free. At best the headstall will break. (Incidentally, apart from in Western riding, tying up by the bridle should be the exception rather than the rule.)

Alternatively, if both headcollar and tie rope are strong and the horse is secured to some flimsy object such as a garden wicket, it will bolt off with this dangling round its forelegs. On one occasion a youngster was tied to the side of a portable cattle crush. The horse pulled back, toppling the crush onto itself and during its subsequent struggles sustained fatal injuries.

Furthermore, when the horse is tied to an immovable object such as a tree there is a risk that in its panic the horse will throw itself down, thereby injuring the pelvic regions. Conversely, it may pull its neck out of line. This misalignment of the atlas and axis bones impairs the future usefulness of the horse, as it will thereafter have little or no lateral suppleness.

To avoid such breaks and injuries, most manuals recommend that a piece of string is attached to the object onto which the horse is tethered and the lead rope tied to this. The string, being the weakest point, will then break first. Old fashioned binder twine made of sisal or cheap parcel string made of hemp or twisted paper are the only variety to use. Modern baling string or similar, of the polyester family, will not break easily enough.

A horse standing tied by this method is proof that its training is complete, the string breaking in the thousand-to-one chance of something frightening the horse into pulling away.

Figure 4 shows the tack on the horse for its first lessons in tying up. In the absence of a good sized ring on the headcollar itself, one must be attached to ensure the rope runs freely. The rope goes between the forelegs and is fastened to a strong roller. Use of a woollen sleeve will prevent galling on thin-skinned horses.

Figure 4 *Tack for teaching the horse to tie up*

For the first lessons the horse must not be tied to any object, but have the trainer as the tethering post. If the horse has previously acquired the habit of breaking loose, it will fight violently to succeed again. An assistant close at hand will lend extra weight if and when required. A rolled up paper bag is then held as shown in figure 5. The gently flapping paper will provoke the horse to pull back. At the same time it safeguards against accidental injury to the eyes, which could happen if the lunge-whip were carried and the horse furiously threw its head about.

If the horse pulls back in a straight line the trainer should slightly bend their knees and allow the horse to pull them along. (If held by brute force, the horse would throw itself down as previously mentioned.) Sooner or later it will come to a halt, when the trainer will tuck the paper bag under their arm, quietly walk to the horse, and make much of it.

The horse should never be allowed to come towards the trainer, but should stand with a light contact on the lead rein, otherwise difficulties will arise when lunging lessons begin.

Figure 5 *Horse backing away from flapping paper*

Figure 6 *Horse walking forward behind trainer*

When, by frequent repetition, the horse no longer runs back at the provocation of the paper bag, it is asked to walk forward behind the trainer. Care is taken that the horse maintains contact at all times, stopping when the trainer stops and moving forwards to a gradually increased pull on the lead rein. The paper bag held directly in front of the horse can be flapped if necessary to ensure that contact is preserved (figure 6).

Some horses acquire the habit of pulling away, by first taking a few steps towards their tethering post and then turning alongside with their head between their legs. They then pull from the poll as opposed to the nose, and in going forwards gather

Figure 7 *Tack for countering pulling from poll*

terrific strength, breaking loose from an immovable tethering post, or dragging the trainer along if he has hold of the rope. It is now that the assistant's extra poundage is of value.

The tack in figure 7 is suitable for counteracting this evasion. Young horses with a natural one-sidedness will only try to get away on the stiff side (see Glossary page 105), therefore the rope is added on that side. This acts in the same manner as a pulley block and doubles the strength of the trainer in ratio to that of the horse. On the other hand the hardened sinner who has successfully resisted numerous attempts to overcome this evasion, will try to evade on either side.

This type of animal is extremely dangerous, because if it feels the trainer being towed along it will break into a gallop. A rein should be attached on each side (each one attached back to the roller in the manner illustrated for the single rein in figure 7), the assistant holding one and the trainer the other. Great care must be taken that the lead ropes are held correctly in the hand (see figure 8) and can be released in an emergency, as fatal accidents have resulted from people being dragged by tangled lead ropes.

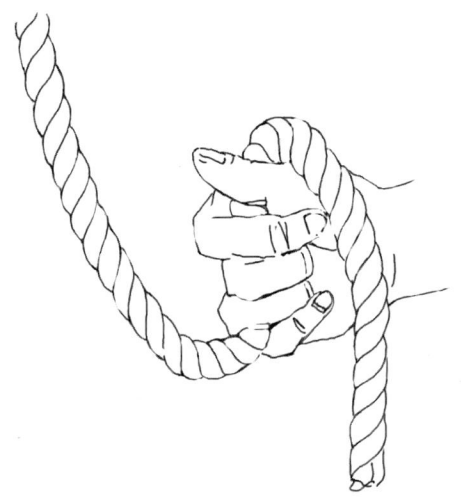

Figure 8 *Correct way to hold a lead rope*

Whenever the trainer is handling a lunge rein or a long rope they must be meticulous in having it properly coiled. For example, if the trainer intends to hold the rope in their left hand, it is temporarily laid across the right hand held palm uppermost and the spare rope coiled loosely over the outstretched fingers. It is then transferred to the left hand, where it can fall freely as and when the trainer wishes.

If it is held in an untidy way, it will soon become entangled to a such a degree that the trainer will be unable to loose it if that should become necessary in an emergency. There have been occasions where horses have bolted, and a person holding a rope incorrectly has suffered serious injuries through being dragged along.

Because the object of the exercise is to train the horse to tie up, any attempt on its part to gallop round on the lunge is stopped by the person who has no contact on the rein waving the paper bag in front of it. If the handlers keep close enough together, they can prevent the horse rushing between them. The horse will eventually stop or change direction. The trainer and assistant then change their roles of restrainer and bag waver.

A series of repetitive lessons are required before the renegade equine condescends to stand. Intermittently, it may resort to pulling back, in which case the tactics described for the first lesson are applied.

Figure 9 *Lead rope threaded through ring and horse pulling back*

An old cow chain or something similar is now fastened to one or another solid object around the premises. The lead rope (at least 20 feet long) is put on the horse as in figure 9. Thread the loose end through the ring and walk away until the pupil is snubbed short enough to the tethering post to prevent it from getting a foreleg over the rope.

Provocation by waving an umbrella or the like can be used to induce the horse to try and pull free. As before, give a little if it pulls straight back and resist strongly if it tries to rush forwards.

This lesson well learned, (figure 10) the horse is then tied to the breakable string by a rack chain or lead rope from the headcollar (figure 11). If it deliberately breaks the string, the education is insufficient and a return to previous lessons is made.

Figure 10 *Horse standing quietly*

Figure 11 *Horse standing tied up*

When the horse is finally left tied up, care should be taken that the ring is high enough and the lead rope short enough to prevent the horse from getting a foreleg over the rope.

If there is need to feed the horse from a receptacle at ground level, the lead rope should be threaded through a ring at breast height and tied to a log of wood called a manger block. This is either square or spherical and rises and falls as the horse lifts and lowers its head, thus ensuring the rope is in light contact with the headcollar at all times. It was in common use when most horses were stabled in stalls as opposed to modern day loose boxes.

If the method above is used, the breakable string should be between the headcollar ring and the lead rope clip.

A horse systematically trained to tie up accepts its lunge lessons more willingly, therefore time taken on this is saved at a later stage.

Chapter Three
The Intractable Horse

No matter how well mannered a horse is in allowing itself to be groomed, it will often resist having the occasional thing done to it, such as tail and mane pulling, dressing minor wounds or galls, clipping, or having a hypodermic injection.

For the sake of safety and expediency, Veterinary Surgeons make use of tranquillisers, or local or general anaesthetics, when handling sick or injured horses. However, they must first get the horse sufficiently passive to put the hypodermic needle directly into the vein. Injected into the muscle by mistake, the drug takes around twenty minutes to have its full effect, and in the interim period the horse staggers round in a comatose state, a danger to itself and its handlers.

Where a restraint is only required for a minute or so, the almost universal method is the stick twitch, which when twisted tight on the upper lip causes the horse so much discomfort in that region that it ignores things being done on other parts of the body. Left on too tight for too long a period, it acts the same as a tourniquet and can do irreparable damage to the horse's muzzle.

Controversy has raged in the past, and still continues to rage, over the humaneness of this method of restraint. In recent years a T.V. documentary justified the use of the stick twitch by claiming it had a hypnotic effect on the patient rather than inflicting pain. As the horse cannot speak, it is debatable whether the truth will ever be known. What we do know, however, is that the more often the stick twitch is used, the shyer will the horse become of having its muzzle touched.

When restraint is needed over a longer period for such things as clipping, mane and tail pulling, or shoeing for the first time, what is known as the Comanche bridle is, in the writer's opinion, a more humane method of restraint. It only needs to be brought into requisition when a horse shows resentment at being handled. When the horse is submissive to whatever is being done to it, the pressure of the rope is relaxed. This adheres to the basic principle of horse-training which has stood the test of time since one of the first treatises of horsemanship was written by Xenophon around 400 B.C., namely that the Comanche bridle provides comfort for a positive response and discomfort for a negative one.

Figure 12 illustrates a simple Comanche bridle adapted from an ordinary headcollar. It is merely a cord tied to the offside of the headcollar, passed under the upper lip

Cord tied to the upper offside ring of the headcollar, passed under the upper lip......

...and threaded through one of the headcollar rings on the nearside.

Figure 12 *The Comanche bridle*

and threaded through one of the headcollar rings on the nearside. There are quite a few variations of this method of restraint which most people could improvise with whatever equipment is available at the time.

When it is necessary to do something around the hindquarters of a young and nervous horse, a foreleg is usually held up on the principle that it is difficult but

Pinching the tendons between knee and fetlock.....

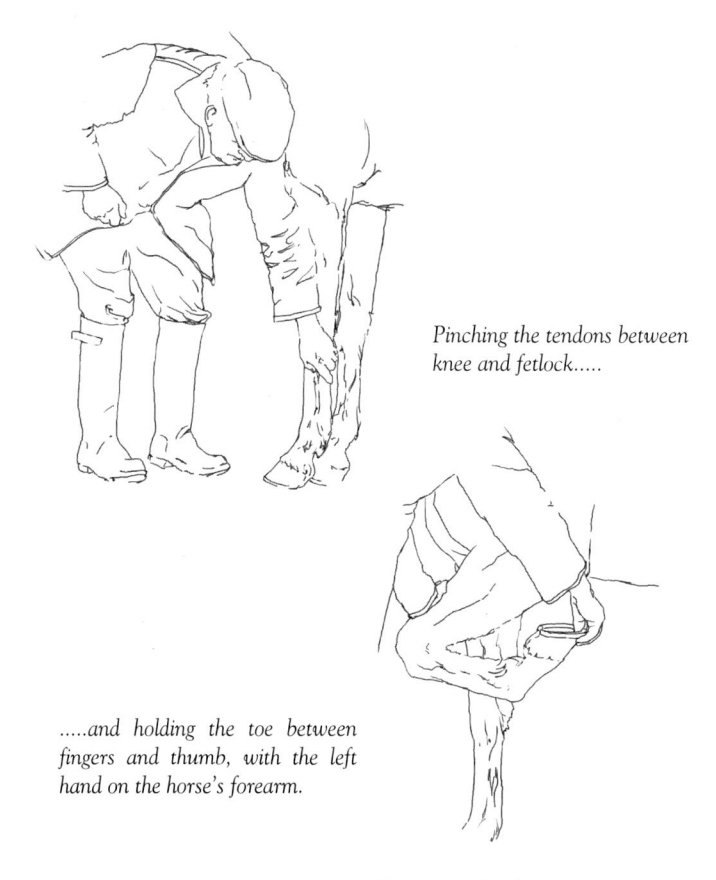

.....and holding the toe between fingers and thumb, with the left hand on the horse's forearm.

Figure 13 *Holding up a foreleg*

not impossible for a horse to kick whilst balancing on the remaining two. If an assistant holds the foreleg off the ground on the same side as the person is working, the restraint is more reliable as it is harder for the horse to balance with a lateral pair of legs in support than a diagonal pair.

Nevertheless, the horse may adopt the ploy of putting the full weight of its flexed foreleg on the assistant holding it, thus enabling it to kick freely with a hind leg. For this reason the old time horse-tamers strapped the foreleg in suspension to ensure the horse stood in self carriage. This was all right with docile heavy horses but is not recommended for the well-bred riding horses of today. Feeling themselves securely fastened, these spirited equines will fight like demons, sometimes throwing themselves down and causing untold injury.

The following method is safer and more humane. Assuming that the near fore is to be picked up, the handler stands facing the rear on that side. With his left hand he pinches the tendons between the knee and the fetlock - the exact place varies with every horse. As the horse lifts its foot to get rid of the irritation, the right hand catches the toe with the first two fingers and the thumb. Immediately, the left hand is placed on the horse's forearm just above the knee.

Provided it does not hop along too violently, the leg can be held in that position indefinitely. The horse will soon get tired of trying to free itself and will stand quietly in self carriage. Figure 13 illustrates this method of holding the foreleg up by the first two fingers and thumb.

If in the initial struggles the horse does hop perilously close to some object, or onto a hard slippery surface, the leg can be quickly released and the horse led back to safe ground.

Whatever the reason for handling the horse, be it for stable management or equitation, the golden rule is to neither hold by brute force nor be so light handed as to let the horse get free. In other words, restrain rather than hold.

Chapter Four
Thoughts on Lungeing

An acquaintance of mine once said that inexperienced persons should not be allowed to lunge young horses. He based his contention on the assumption that incorrect lungeing was the fertile cause of many types of unsoundness in the green youngster: namely sore-shins, splints, curby hocks and sprained tendons. Bad lungeing can also lead to such injuries as over-reaches, speedy-cuttings and bruising. On the other hand, correct lungeing has so many advantages that every conscientious horseman should be acquainted with its principles.

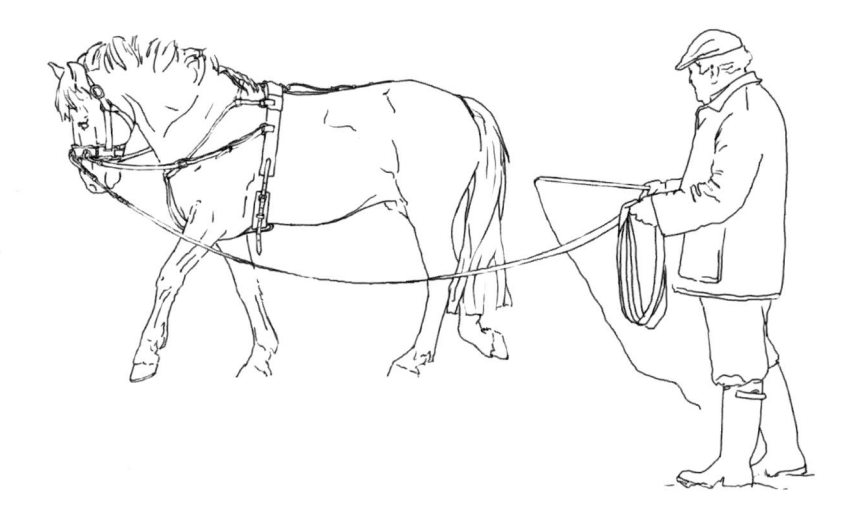

Figure 14 *Showing triangle of lunge rein, horse and whip*

Lungeing correctly carried out supples the young horse and gets him fit prior to backing. It also disciplines both young and older equines that are over-fresh. It is also a good form of exercise for the horse who, through a minor indisposition of himself or the trainer, cannot be ridden for a few days. In thinking how best I can explain to the tyro lunge trainer the method of lungeing which I practise, I offer the following observations to my readers as 'Thoughts on Lungeing'.

Not only in lungeing, but all through the training of the horse, there are certain golden rules we should keep in the back of our minds. Firstly, we must realise that we cannot force our horse to do anything he does not want to do, but that if we oppose him in evading our requests he will eventually do what we have asked of him. This is the time to relax all whip and rein aids and reward him by temporarily ceasing all work.

After a prolonged session of opposing the horse's evasions, which might well be violent, both horse and trainer will be exhausted; so as soon as the horse shows the least inclination to do what is asked of him we should return him to his stable or paddock for a complete rest. He may be got out once or twice later in the day to confirm what has been taught, as short lessons at frequent intervals are more beneficial than long lessons at less frequent intervals.

Secondly, our training programme should be a sequence of lessons, each one being a preparation for the next. Whenever difficulties are being encountered it is better to go back to an earlier lesson than to let the horse get the upper hand. With horses that are stabled or over fresh, it is advisable to begin with the very first lesson and go quietly through the sequence as far as the stage of training has reached.

Thirdly, the trainer should never lose his temper. Nevertheless, he must be sufficiently determined to release his adrenalin when it is required in order to combat the more or less violent evasions the horse will put up from time to time. Unlike poodles, horses cannot be trained with sugar, and in the initial stages it is necessary to apply some strong rein aids and energetic driving aids.

Since the ultimate aim is to obtain lightness, the aids should always be applied in the first instance in a tentative way and gradually increased in severity until the desired result has been obtained. When it is required for the horse to be driven forwards, the point of the whip should first touch the ground about a metre behind the horse's hind legs. The next stroke should touch him lightly just above the hocks and each subsequent stroke should gradually increase in severity until he responds. In time, with an occasional refresher course, he will quietly respond to a mere gesture of the whip pointed at his quarters.

Likewise, if the horse suddenly plunges forward with a tough contact on the lunge rein, the straightening of the trainer's arm from the elbow joint will act as a buffer before the horse eventually meets the full force of the handler's weight on the rein. The rein should give as the horse gives, achieving in time a lightness of hand which can control the horse by the opening and closing of the fingers.

Figure 15 *The triangle from the outside*

Our horse will be working well on the lunge when he is moving on a circle twenty metres in diameter at rhythmic paces with his body bent laterally on the track of the circle (figures 14, 15). Ideally the horse's body should form the base of a triangle and the trainer the apex. There should be equal distance from the horse's nose to the trainer's hand as there is from the trainer to the horse's buttocks. The lunge line should never be so long that the whip cannot reach the horse, and he should remain in contact with it at all times.

In fact, as long as the trainer continues to walk forward on a small circle this is proof that the horse is maintaining correct contact with the lunge rein and not falling into the circle. Needless to say, much time and patience will be needed before this ideal is reached.

Lunge training can be divided into roughly two stages, the initial stage being what we have to do when the young horse, through instinctive fear and misunderstanding, puts up a more or less violent resistance; and the later stage when we politely ask a co-operative youngster to perform a sequence of gymnastic exercises which will bring him to a state of physical and mental fitness preparatory to being ridden.

For those who intend to avail themselves of the many advantages of lungeing, the investment in correct equipment is money well spent. In particular, the cavesson

Figure 16 *Cavesson*

(figure 16) is a must. Whilst it may be advantageous to use a strong well fitting headcollar on an unbroken colt that runs back violently, the cavesson offers more control over the horse that puts its head down and rushes off. The roller should be fitted with a breastplate to prevent the girth slipping back towards the hips and causing the horse to buck (figure 17). The roller should also be fitted with a crupper, as otherwise it will gall behind the elbows should the youngster take a fairly strong contact on the side reins.

The side reins should be left reasonably slack at first until it has been found out what the horse's evasions are. (Introducing a horse to side reins for the first time is covered in a later chapter.) Side reins too tightly adjusted have been the cause of many an injury, due to the horse throwing himself down or falling over backwards. These injuries do not always show up at the time of the accident.

I refer to the horse rearing over backwards as an accident because, contrary to a fairly common belief, the trainer should never deliberately pull the horse over. Great tact must be used immediately the youngster shows a tendency to rear, as

Figure 17 *Tack for lungeing without bit*

not only is there a danger of injury or death to the horse should he fall, but the youngster also learns that by rearing he can escape the hand and the seeds of nappiness and rebellion are sown.

The herd instinct of every horse creates a tendency for him to hang towards other horses, the paddock gate or the stable: in other words, to home. This homing instinct should always be in the thoughts of the trainer, who should be ready to combat the evasion each time it occurs. On passing home some horses will try to go there by suddenly swinging their quarters in towards the trainer and either putting their heads down and rushing off, or worse still standing on their hind legs. As I look upon rearing as the more serious evasion of the two, I will deal with that first.

Some authorities advocate hitting the horse across the rump with the lunge whip whenever he rears, on the assumption that if he is driven forward he will answer to the lunge rein and turn whichever way he is being asked to go. On the contrary, I find we already have more impulsion than we can deal with and to create more would only add fuel to the fire. A study of how the classical levade or courbette are obtained will illustrate my point.

Figure 18 *Teaching the rein back*

From experience, I find that horses which rein back or overbend laterally do not rear, so immediately the horse shows an inclination to stand up I set about teaching him the rein back. If later on he uses this newly taught lesson as an evasion, I do not discourage him in the first instance, as I prefer him to use this less violent evasion. Later on I will tentatively ask him to go forward by applying the whip to his quarters as described earlier.

To teach the rein back, I temporarily discard the lunge rein and whip for the shorter in-hand lead rein and cutting whip. In so doing, I practise the great principle of training: that of going back to basic exercises when in difficulty.

Standing on the nearside of the horse with my right shoulder more or less parallel to that of his, I hold the rein in my right hand and tap him across the chest with my cutting whip which I am holding in my left (figure 18). At first he may strike out with either of his forelegs, in which case the lead rein allows me to step out of his way without loosing him.

Alternatively, he may turn his head slightly away from me and push into me with his shoulder, in which case I quickly change the rein into my left hand and place my right hand on his shoulder. By pulling the head towards me with my left hand

and pushing the shoulders away with my right, I leave him with no option but to move his quarters from left to right (figure 19). (These are the first steps of a turn on the forehand which is thought by many authorities to be a good preparation for a rein back.)

Figure 19 *First steps of a turn on the forehand*

When the horse responds willingly to the above exercises I once more try him on the lunge, being content to go back to close work whenever he shows a resistance.

The youngster that puts its head down and rushes off can be quite a nuisance, and if being lunged in an enclosure larger than twenty metres across (or in diameter) will gather speed and get away from the trainer. Therefore in lunge training one should take care to not have the spare rein coiled up in a careless way. When being led or lunged, most horses resist on one side and respond too easily on the other. The horse only attempts to rush off like this when being lunged on its stiff side.

To try to escape in this manner the horse must put his head between his forelegs with his face almost parallel to the ground. He then stiffens his neck and pulls from the poll. With a well fitting cavesson and two persons on the lunge rein this evasion can be nipped in the bud, but if we have the misfortune to be dealing with an animal that has previously been allowed his own way, firm measures must be resorted to. It is recommended by some that the side reins - particularly the inside one - should be somewhat shorter than usual. If the horse has shown a tendency to rear as well as rush off, the tightening of the side reins could be risky.

Figure 20 *Counteracting running off*

I prefer to thread the lunge rein through a fair sized ring clipped to the inside dee of the cavesson on the side on which the horse is stiff and buckled back to the roller as a running rein (figure 20). If the rein is threaded directly through the dee on the cavesson it will not run freely and we shall have the same predicament as with fixed side reins. The running rein with its pulley block action exerts pressure in ratio to the horse's resistance, but can be released immediately if he rears. It also becomes loose when the horse submits to the restraint, thus adhering to the principle of rewarding the horse for obedience.

When being lunged on the soft side in the early stages of breaking, the horse will show yet another violent evasion. On passing the home end of the menage, he will swing his quarters out and run back. If he runs back straight, the trainer will have no difficulty in stopping him within a few steps. However, some cunning animals cultivate the habit of overbending to the inside, and, having established a fairly strong contact on the rein, seem able to move sideways at considerable speed, taking the trainer with them.

Figure 21 Rein attached to soft side

Once again, I prefer to use the running rein as already described for the horse that rushes off, but this time the rein is attached on the horse's soft side (figure 21). It seems impossible for him to take a dead pull on the rein when it is threaded through the ring on the cavesson and if he runs back straight the pull at the girth seems to take him by surprise and he jumps forward.

Until now I have not mentioned putting a bit in the horse's mouth. Up to the point where he can move calmly on a twenty metre circle there is always a danger of his injuring his mouth during one of his more energetic outbursts in the early days of training. Before the addition of the bit, the side reins were attached to the side dees of the cavesson and should have been only sufficiently short as to stop the horse grazing or putting his leg over the lunge rein.

A thick bit should be used in the first instance, preferably a jointed snaffle (figure 22). Care should be taken to ensure that the bit is not too wide, otherwise the centre joint will hang too low and encourage him to get his tongue over the bit. This annoying habit should be promptly nipped in the bud by tying a piece of tape over the centre joint of the bit, bringing the ends out on either side of the mouth and then tying them to the centre dee of the cavesson.

Almost every horse has a hard and a soft side to his mouth, overbending on the soft side and either resisting or turning like a boat on the other (see page 45). Some people believe that horses are born like this, just as humans are left and right handed.

I am of the opinion that the seeds are sown when the horse is first led as a foal. My observations show that most ex-racehorses are stiff on the nearside but horses and ponies that have been shown in hand up to three years old are soft on this side. I attribute this to the fact that stable lads are merely concerned with parading their charges in the paddock on a right hand circle with the minimum of interference to the horse's

Figure 22 *Cavesson with bit*

Figure 23 *Shoulder falling in*

stride; whereas the leaders of in-hand show stock try to present their horses before the judges in a balanced manner. Unfortunately in schooling for this they quite often get their charges overbending to the left.

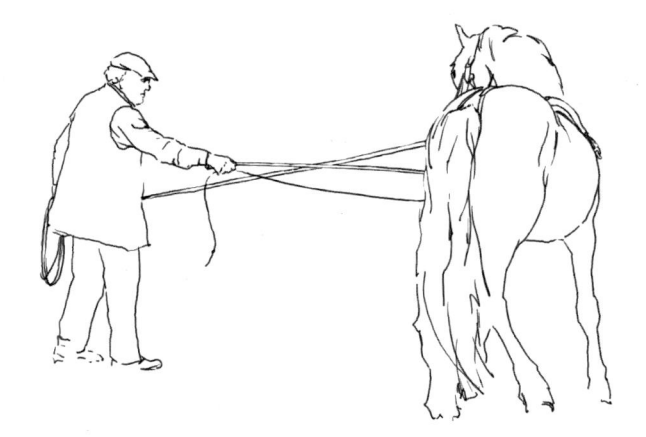

Figure 24 *Whip pointed to shoulder*

Let us imagine that we are dealing with a horse that is hard on the near side. When we are working such a horse on the left rein, he will be looking out and have an inclination to fall into the circle (figure 23). In the first instance he should be touched on the inside shoulder with the lunge whip (figure 24) to ask him to

Figure 25 *Shoulder corrected*

take his shoulders out, and at the same time, by maintaining contact with the rein, we would hope to bend his head, neck, and croup laterally inwards (figure 25). If instead of doing this he increases his pace and races round in an uncontrolled manner, we should stop him and shorten the left side rein (the inside one). He may now turn inwards towards the trainer or even about-turn onto the other rein. We should, however, continue to flick him on the nearside shoulder and he will eventually start to sidestep from left to right in the manner of a rudimentary shoulder-in. At this stage we should reward him by ceasing to flick with the whip, and give with the lunge rein. More often than not he will then take his forehand onto the track and go correctly on the circle.

When working the same horse on the right rein, which is his soft side, he will overbend inwards at the withers. It goes without saying that we must counter this by shortening the outside rein; but, as the outside rein must never be shorter than the inside one, the latter must be adjusted accordingly.

Having got the horse tracking on the circle and established a light contact with the bit, we should concentrate on rhythmic paces: especially at trot. This is done by vibrating the lunge if the tempo is too fast and driving on with the whip at the quarters when the pace is too slow. Just as there must be a co-ordination between hand and leg in riding, so must the lunge maintain contact to receive and distribute the impulsion created by the driving whip. Conversely, the whip must be kept close to the quarters ready to keep the hocks underneath the horse as the lunge rein slows the tempo.

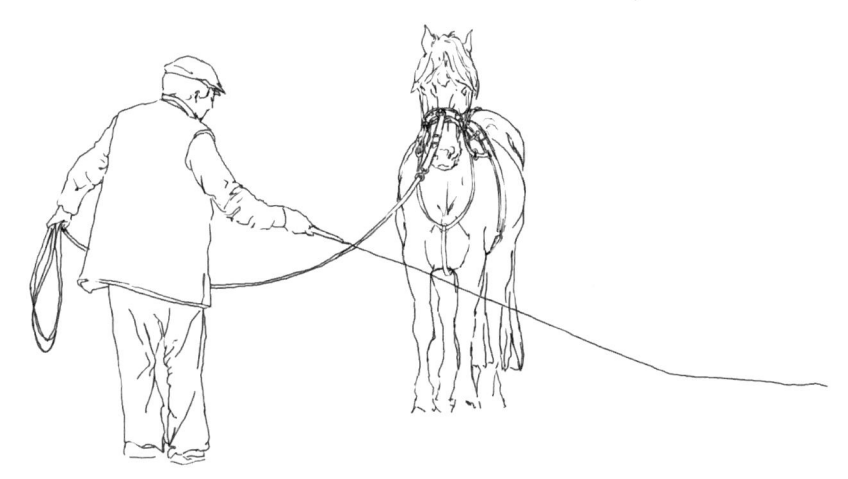

Figure 26 *Whip and rein changed over*

To change the rein, I bring the horse to the walk and, whilst he is still on the track, I change the whip and rein into opposite hands. For an example, if the horse is on the right rein I shall now have my whip in my right hand and the rein in my left (figure 26). As already explained on page 20, the lead rope must be checked frequently and coiled correctly as it changes from one hand to the other. This guards against it getting entangled in the trainer's legs with disastrous results.

On the command 'Change', I put my hand holding the rein out to the left as far as it will go and simultaneously send the lash of the whip across the horse's breast for the point to touch him on the nearside shoulder, when the trained horse will change (figure 27).

Figure 27 *Horse turning in response*

Through lack of understanding in the initial stages, the youngster will not do as he is asked, in which case we must put down the whip, coil up the lunge and go close to the horse. Our right hand on the left hand side of the horse's muzzle should ask him to move from left to right (figure 28). If he only moves his head away instead of his whole body, we should run our right hand down his neck and push his shoulders away from us. We should then allow him to walk on and gradually pay out the lunge until we are back towards the centre where we can pick up the whip and proceed as before.

Physical fitness and ground conditions both being suitable, it is beneficial for future training under the rider if the horse is taught to strike off in canter equally on both leads. Quite often a young horse will strike off with the wrong leg, especially on the rein upon which he has a tendency to overbend to the inside. This is because the faulty bending at the withers overloads the inside shoulder, thereby making it difficult for him to lead with that leg.

We should profit by this knowledge and ensure the outside rein is sufficiently short to prevent the inside shoulder from becoming overloaded. As the horse passes the wall of the school, we should give with the rein and simultaneously apply the driving aids to the quarters. The wall will prevent him from swinging his quarters out and the giving of the rein will encourage him to lighten the inside shoulder.

On the opposite rein, which will be his stiff side, he will naturally have his shoulder free and will break into canter quite easily. Therefore, practise the most on the lazy lead (the soft side).

Figure 28 *Turning the green horse, hand on muzzle*

Those who assiduously lunge are not only rewarded by the general improvement of outline and paces of the horse, but become so absorbed with the work that it becomes an equestrian art in itself.

Chapter Five
Introducing Side Reins

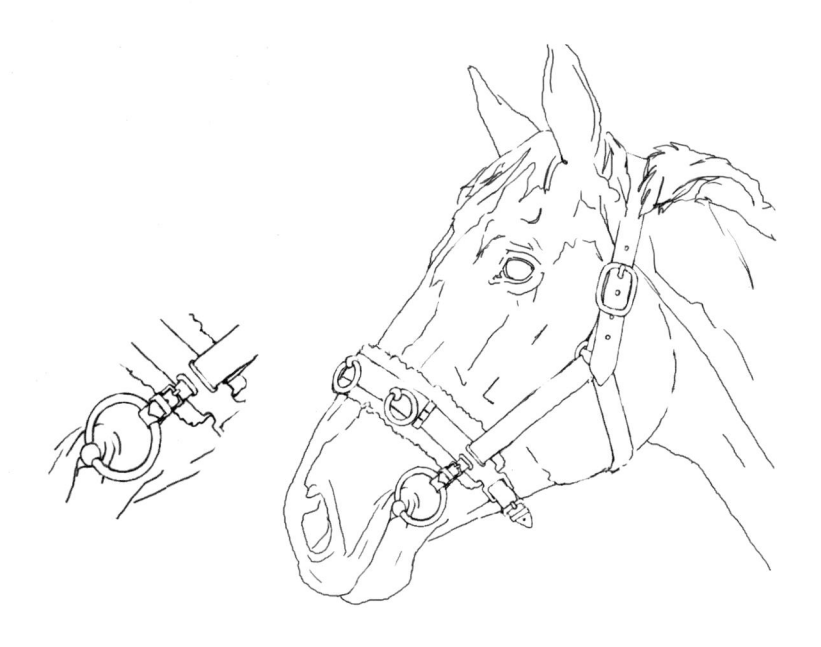

Figure 29 *Bit attached with bit straps*

A trained horse working calmly on the lunge with correctly adjusted side reins is a joy to watch, but it is when training the young horse to accept the right contact and outline on these reins that accidents happen or the seeds of evasions are sown.

Unlike riding, long reining, or driving in harness, the side reins of a lunge horse are fixed and cannot be loosened in an emergency. It is invariably advised that they are adjusted with great circumspection. Even then, with untrained horses, it is difficult to find the lengths that are suitable. One minute the side reins are too slack, enabling the horse to put its head between its legs and rush off. If they are then tightened up a couple of holes, the youngster rears up and falls over backwards, risking injured vertebrae or a broken neck. A safe method of getting a horse to accept the side reins is described below.

Assuming the horse is used to wearing various equipment in the stable, it is tacked up in the orthodox lunging gear minus the side reins. A crupper and breastplate or breast girth will prevent the roller from moving forwards or backwards. Likewise, a rubber or thick snaffle is attached to the cavesson by bit straps as opposed to a separate bridle (figure 29). Its main purpose is to prevent the cavesson noseband working up too high, thus reducing control.

Figure 30 *Grass reins fitted*

At this stage some youngsters acquire the habit of getting the tongue over the bit. Most authorities advocate that the bit is fastened higher in the mouth. If this does not succeed, dropping the bit lower than average may have the desired effect. The theory is that a horse has no difficulty in getting the tongue over the bit, but great trouble getting it back.

Whilst still in the stable, a cord is loosely attached between the bit rings through the centre ring of the roller as illustrated in figure 30. (This is sometimes known as a grass rein.) This will prevent the horse from putting its head too low and stepping over the lunge rein. (Youngsters should be constantly watched while wearing tack in the stable, as they often find some protrusion on which to get the tack entangled. The result is broken equipment or a frightened horse.)

Figure 31 *Rein attached to stiff side*

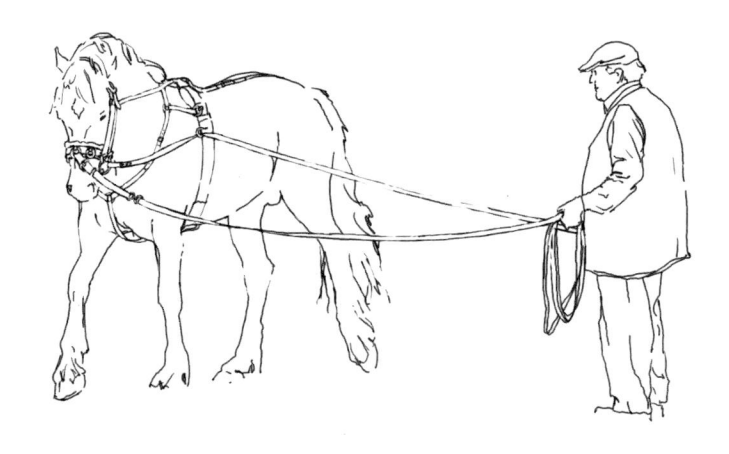

Figure 32 *Horse going calmly*

The horse is taken into an enclosed school and lunged a few times to either hand in the usual manner. This is for the trainer to establish which is the horse's stiff side. If it turns its head to the outside and falls into the circle, it is stiff on the inside. On the opposite rein - the horse's soft side - it will overbend at the withers to the inside and make the circle larger.

Assuming the horse is resisting - i.e. is stiff - on the left rein, a second lunge rein is attached to the left ring on the cavesson and threaded through the ring on the roller, making sure it runs freely (figure 31). The lunge whip is dispensed with, as the trainer will require a hand for each rein. Figure 32 is a view of the horse going calmly with both reins in contact.

If the horse falls in to the circle, a stronger pressure on the introductory side rein will ask for more bend to the inside, thus causing the youngster to side-step back onto track and take contact with the lunge rein proper.

However, through misunderstanding, the horse may turn to the left and attempt to change the rein. The introductory side rein will discourage the horse from coming in to the trainer. Figure 33 shows this evasion. By flicking the introductory side rein on the horse's shoulder whilst maintaining a steady contact, the horse will

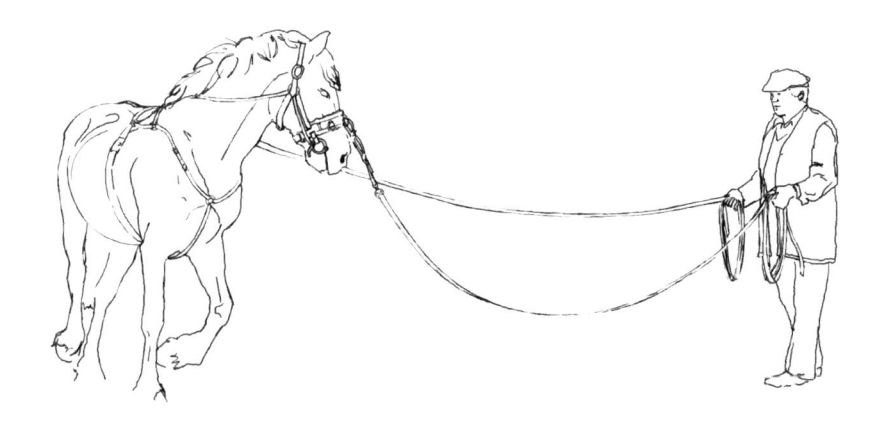

Figure 33 *Horse mistakenly attempting to change rein*

Figure 34 *Returning to proper track*

Figure 35 *Running back*

Figure 36 *Introductory rein over back when lungeing on soft side*

return to the proper track (figure 34). If the youngster runs back, (figure 35) it can easily be restrained - the pull being on the roller and crupper rather than the head. Only if the horse attempts to rear are both reins loosened.

When working on the right rein, which is this horse's soft side, the introductory side rein is passed over the horse's back and becomes the outside rein (see figure 36). If the horse falls out, trying to make the circle larger, the introductory side rein will prevent an over-bending of the neck to the inside, which causes the shoulder to fall out. As before, any halting or running back is countered by the trainer shortening the lunge rein proper and walking forward.

Needless to say, for an horse that resists on the right rein, the introductory side rein is attached on that side.

When the horse goes willingly forward to either rein on a large circle, maintaining even contact on both the lunge rein and the introductory side rein, the orthodox side reins can be fitted with safety.

The whip is then taken up and normal lunge training commences.

Chapter Six
Thoughts on Long Reining

One of the advantages of long reining is that a young horse's education can be taken much farther than lunging in side reins. With no weight on its back, and without the need to work in small circles, the young horse can be worked at an earlier age than its immature bones would stand if it were ridden. Long reins - as

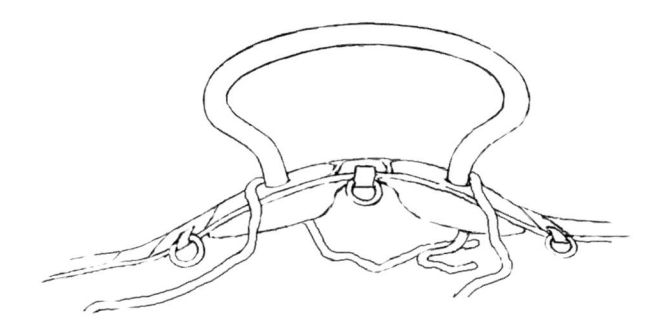

Figure 37 Long reining saddle, author's version

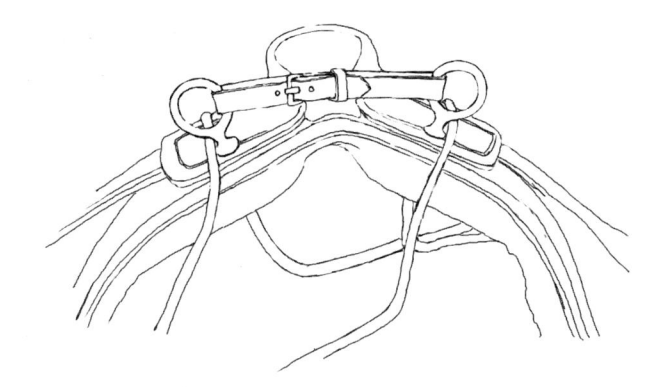

Figure 38 Driving pad adapted for use as a long reining saddle

opposed to side reins - can be loosened if the youngster attempts to rear, or contact increased if the he tries to rush off. If an older horse is unable to be ridden for any reason, its schooling can continue in long reins. Some people practise long reining up to high school work.

Figure 39 *Long reining gear*

The long reining saddle, or a driving pad (figures 37, 38) is introduced to the horse in the stable. When a driving pad is used, it is beneficial to fasten a strap between the rein terrets as illustrated. This prevents the rein getting entangled with the rings and the trainer losing control of the horse.

A lungeing cavesson is fitted, to which a mild bit is attached by bit strap. Grass reins are put on, which should only be tight enough to prevent the horse getting its head down to graze. They should run freely through a ring on the driving pad, thus enabling the horse to bend laterally (figure 39).

The long reins are attached to the noseband of the cavesson in the early stages. If the youngster leans heavily on the reins and tries to rush off, they must be attached to the bit. In general, rubber bits or double or single jointed snaffles are suitable for horses that are reluctant to take contact, and a thick half moon or straight bar snaffle often persuades the youngster to relax its lower jaw and go forward without leaning. In the initial training, the reins should never be threaded through the loops in a driving pad. As the young horse has previously been led in hand, it will invariably try to turn towards its trainer, thereby getting entangled in the reins.

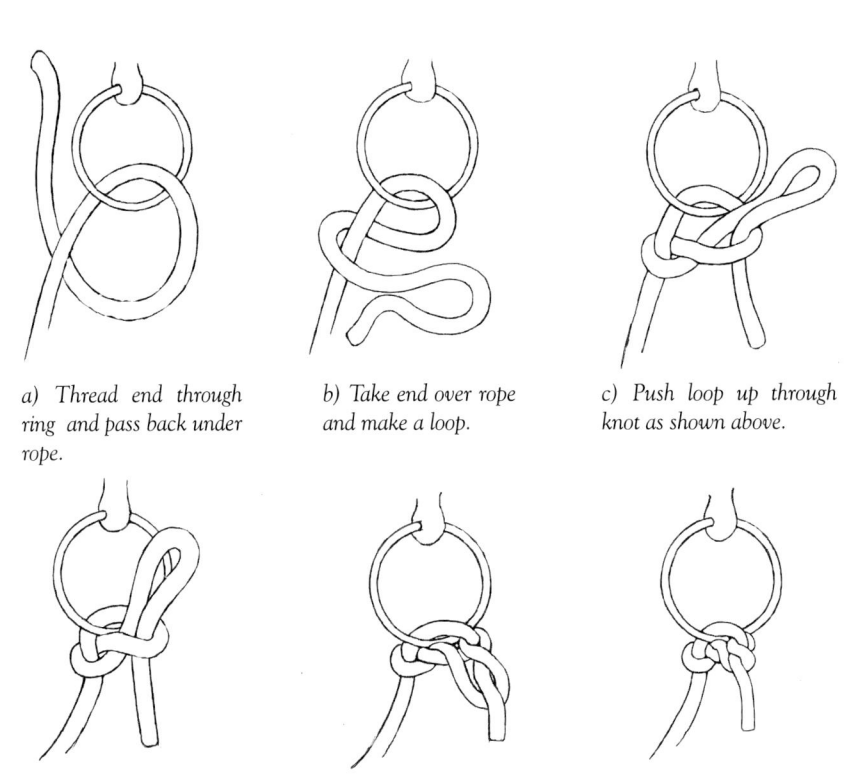

a) Thread end through ring and pass back under rope.

b) Take end over rope and make a loop.

c) Push loop up through knot as shown above.

d) Pull loop and rope firmly to form knot. At this stage, pulling the end will release the knot.

e) For security, pass end through loop.

f) Pull end and rope to secure knot. To undo, take end, pass back through loop and pull; it will loose as in d).

Figure 40 *Tying a plough rope to a ring*

The author finds that using the lungeing whip in conjunction with webbing reins is cumbersome. He prefers to use rope plough reins, or ordinary rope of similar weight (figure 40). With these one can apply a strong enough driving aid by flicking one or the other rein alongside the horse's flank. This is like an individual leg aid and prepares for that in later mounted training.

Training should begin on a circle, with the inside rein coming direct to the trainer's hand as in lungeing. The outside rein is passed over the horse's back and behind the loop on the driving pad (figure 41). As the horse circles around the trainer, the outside rein should play its correct role in equitation of controlling the pace

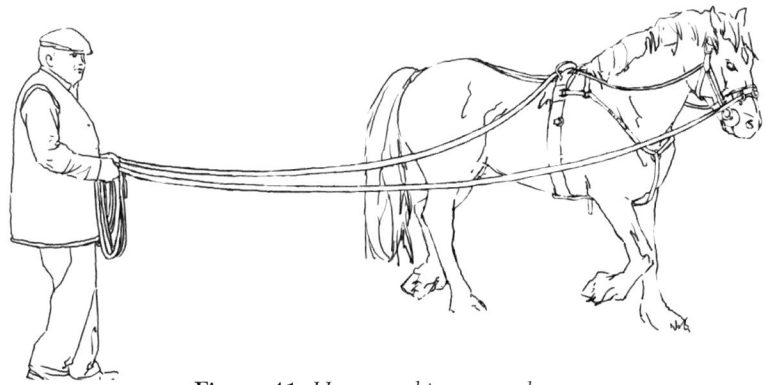

Figure 41 *Horse working correctly*

and preventing the neck from over-bending to the inside. The inside rein plays the role of an exaggerated open rein - similar to that used when riding - thus giving the horse a sense of direction.

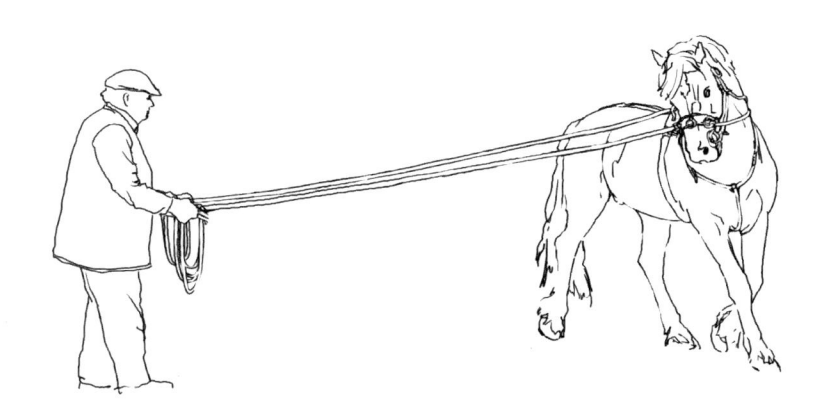

Figure 42 *Falling out on the lunge (shoulder-in evasion)*

Invariably, a young horse will soon find out how to escape contact. Assuming it is stiff on the left side and soft on the right, the youngster will overbend to the inside and swing its quarters to the outside when going in a clockwise direction, thus 'falling out' (putting itself in shoulder-in position) as an evasion (figures 42, 43).

b) *Horse now going correctly; quarters, head and neck following the circle. The outside rein round the quarters brings the hindlegs back to the track.*

a) *Horse 'falling out'; i.e. overbending or 'rubbernecking' to the inside, with shoulders moving on a circle inside that of the quarters, thereby putting itself in a crude shoulder-in position.*
This is also known as falling out through the shoulder. The horse will be moving out of the circle, and will be pulling on the lunge line.

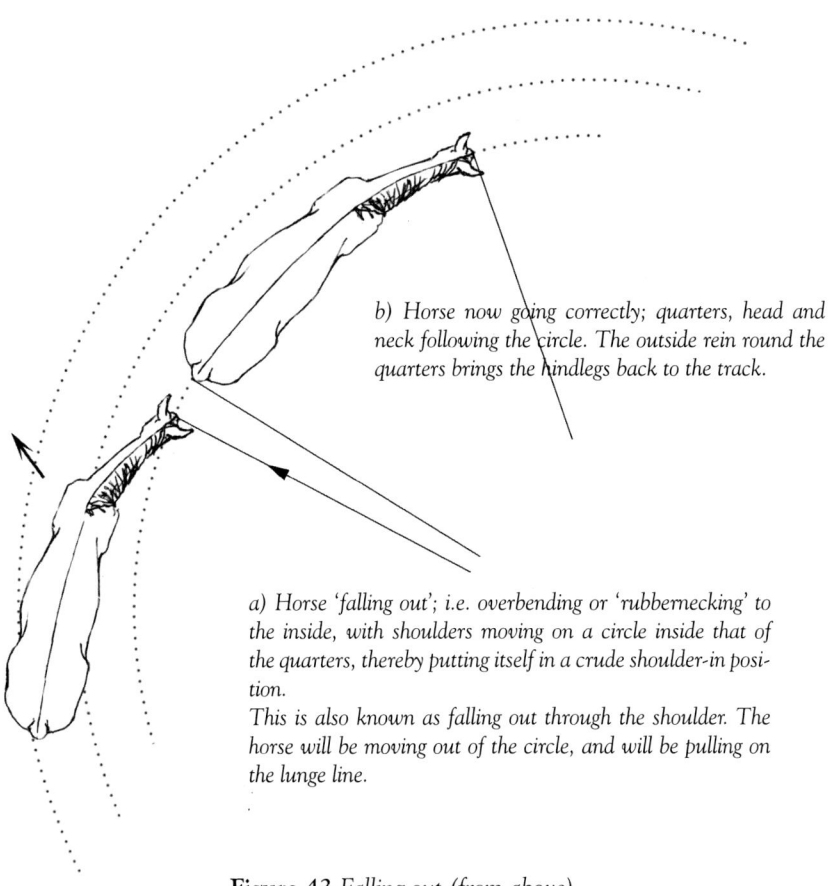

Figure 43 *Falling out (from above)*

Conversely, in an anticlockwise direction the same horse will turn its head to the outside and carry its quarters in; 'falling in' (doing a rudimentary shoulder-out), whilst at the same time getting behind the bit (figures 44, 45).

To counter the latter evasion, the inside rein is vibrated until the horse goes out on the correct track of the circle and takes contact with the inside rein (figure 46). If the trainer is inexperienced, an assistant should persuade the youngster to sidestep back to track by pushing on its inside shoulder. The trainer continues to vibrate the inside rein, which will ask the horse to bend its head inwards. This will also prevent the horse from being tempted to rush past the assistant, cow-kicking as it goes.

Figure 44 *Falling in on the lunge (shoulder-out evasion)*

b) Here the horse is going correctly, with the quarters, shoulders and neck all moving on the same circle.

a) Horse 'falling in' to the centre of the circle, head turned to the outside. The shoulders are moving on a larger circle than the quarters, thereby doing an elementary 'shoulder-out'. This is also known as falling in through the shoulder. The horse is also 'behiud the bit' and the lead rein will be slack.

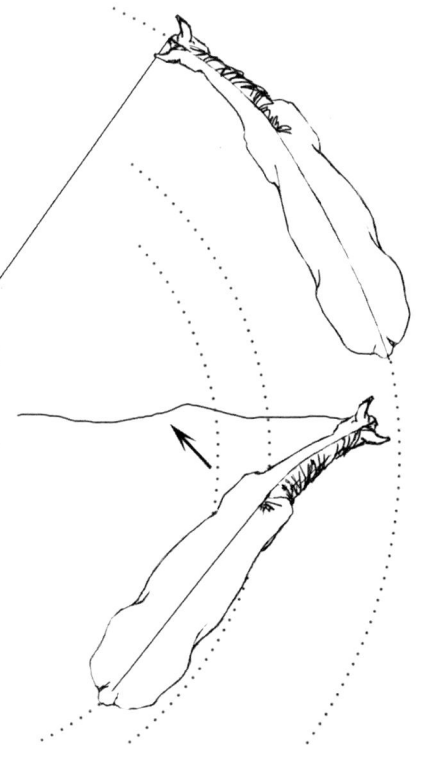

Figure 45 *Falling in (from above)*

Figure 46 *Counteracting falling in (shoulder-out evasion)*

On the opposite (right) rein, where the horse overbends inwards and carries its quarters out, the outside rein must be placed round the quarters to persuade the horse to bring its hind legs onto the proper track (figure 47). Most horses kick

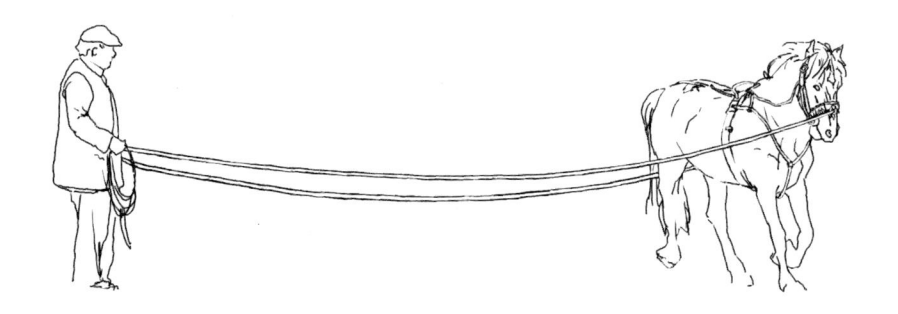

Figure 47 *Counteracting falling out (shoulder-in evasion)*

violently when first feeling the rein in that position. Care must be taken that any loose ends of the reins are properly coiled and can be quickly let go should they get below the hocks. Most youngsters soon settle down to the reins behind the buttocks and start to go forward with a steady contact.

54

Gradually the horse is taught to change direction by turning outwards and a correct contact established on the other circle. Little by little the changes become more frequent until they are done after every half circle. This is the first stage of driving in a straight line. When the stage of driving in straight lines has been reached, the horse is just short of submission: that is to say, it should relax the lower jaw to the pressure of the bit and come into outline (flex longitudinally)

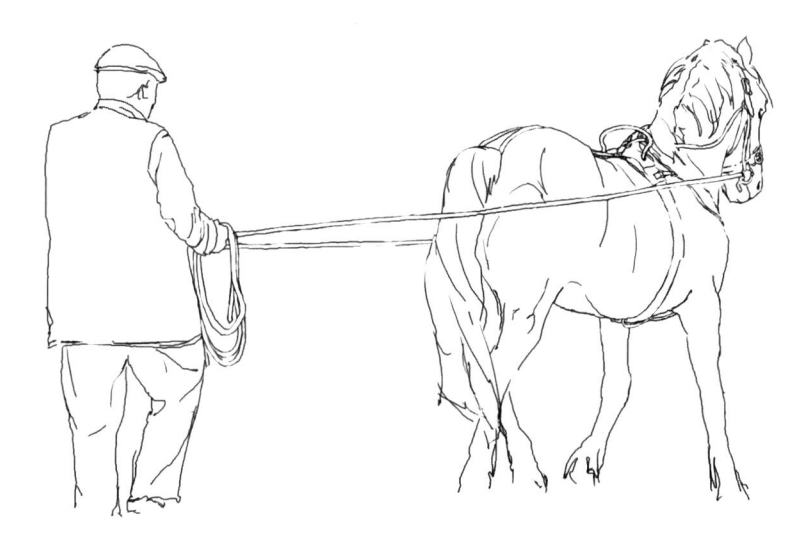

Figure 48 *Driving in a straight line, the horse just short of submission*

(see figure 48). Because young horses have not learned to relax the lower jaw in the initial stages of long reining, they will sooner or later try to escape contact with the bit. If they run back, the trainer should also walk back, maintaining the contact at least on the stiff side until the horse gets fed up and walks forward or at least stands still.

Driving aids should be very tactful, especially if the youngster is reluctant to turn away from home (i.e. he 'naps' - see Glossary, page 105). In this case, circling should be recommenced with the outside rein over the horse's back and behind the loop on the long reining pad. When the horse goes freely forward, driving on straight lines can be tried once more.

Frequently the trainer - quite correctly - applies a strong driving aid on the opposite side to the rein that is being resisted. The trained horse responds by going forward into its bridle and relaxing the lower jaw, but the increased impulsion in a green horse may provoke it to rear. As the trainer is obliged to relax the reins, to avoid pulling the horse over backwards, the horse takes this as a reward and inadvertently an evasion has been taught.

Immediately the horse shows an inclination to rear, driving in straight lines should be temporarily abandoned and as always the basic training on a 20 metre circle resorted to.

Figure 49 *Side-stepping*

By varying the work from straight lines to circles and back to straight lines the youngster will become more supple laterally and longitudinally. It will relax in its lower jaw and take a fairly even contact with both reins.

Side-stepping to and from the wall can be practised, although this will be shown more easily as leg-yields than half-passes (figure 49). Canter strike-offs can also be obtained on the circle bearing in mind the horse's tendency to fall into the circle. This is countered by applying the principles laid down earlier in this chapter.

Figure 50 *Long reining down a quiet lane.*

Chapter Seven
Thoughts on Schooling
Part 1 : The Basic Principles

Free Forward Movement

The horse moving freely forward is the *sine qua non* of all schooling. Willingness to move forward to the rider's driving aids must take precedence over all other lessons. After a period of rest from training, most horses with any "pluck" will test the rider's authority when work is resumed, by not going freely forward. Hence the necessity to warm up before jumping competitions and ride-in before dressage tests.

Whenever the horse shows a tendency to slow down or get behind the bit it must be driven forward with great energy until it accepts contact with the rein aids and once more goes freely forward. The ideal state of affairs is when the horse moves forward to a light application of the leg aids and responds lightly to restraining rein aids.

Achieving this is a long and arduous job. It will be preceded by intermittent phases of the horse either requiring driving forward with great energy into an almost imperceptible contact or the contact being too strong and the horse trying to rush off. At the same time the head will be carried either too high or too low.

Schooling to the Aids

Aids are a combination of signals the rider gives to the horse to ask it to do something. By repetition the horse will in time respond to the lightest of these aids. Basically the rider's legs control the horse's hindquarters and the reins the forehand. It is the co-ordination of rein and leg in a variety of ways which enables the rider to school their horse to do whatever they require it to do.

A leg applied on the girth is a driving aid, asking the horse to go forward. Alternatively, a leg a hand's breadth behind the girth is a pushing aid, either asking the horse to move its hindquarters away from the leg, or restraining it from throwing its haunches to that side.

The rein aids receive and distribute the impulsion created by the legs and when carried either to the left or the right either ask the horse to change direction or counter any deviation he makes from the track the rider requires him to go on. A single rein aid asks for a lateral bend in that direction or restrains the horse from over-bending the opposite way.

From a 'bird's eye view' there should be a straight line from the rider's elbow via the rein to the horse's mouth except when the reins are carried to the left or right, and even then the hands should remain the same distance apart. The hand that is carried outwards is called an open rein and the wrist is turned fingernails uppermost, as otherwise the elbow comes away from the body. Care must be taken that the rein of opposition carried towards the opposite hip does not cross the withers. Not only would this be penalised in Equitation classes, but it is ineffective as an aid as it only restrains if held towards the opposite hip.

Needless to say, the rein of opposition is unnecessary on the horse's soft side, as is also the open rein on the stiff side, as the horse progresses in its training the carrying of the reins to left or right will be almost imperceptible.

Since we cannot force a horse to do anything he does not want to do, we can only ask him to do what we would like and oppose him doing what he wants to do.

For example: a nappy horse refuses to go away from home. He is attacked with whip and spur in an irrational manner and often becomes more violent. Alternatively, we could passively restrain him with the rein aids from gaining ground towards home, when more often than not he will get fed up and turn in the direction we want. If the hands are lightened at this moment, he will take it as a reward and the rider has achieved the first lesson in free forward movement.

Aids are an association of ideas to which the horse is gradually taught to respond. Through a sequence of exercises, in which each lesson prepares the horse for the next, he is slowly built up to a state of physical and mental fitness which allows him to respond to almost imperceptible aids.

The hands must only receive and distribute the amount of impulsion created by the legs. Therefore first lessons must be obedience to them, but contrary to common belief the reins should not be slack, as, in this state, the nervous youngster is in a position to buck and the lethargic animal will stop or change direction at the lightest touch of a rein. The latter is behind the bit, and if allowed to work in this manner will not only prematurely wear out his forelegs, but will also be a miserable ride, as his rider has no control over balance or pace.

The aim is to have a horse whose hind legs are sufficiently under him to propel himself along. This is referred to as balance or horizontal equilibrium and can only be achieved if the horse is kept straight, that is to say straight in long lines, and neither overbent nor underbent laterally when working in circles. He is kept straight by the co-ordination of hands and legs. The horse moving on a long rein

Figure 51 *Horse moving correctly on a long rein*

and stretching is the result of schooling and not the beginning. He should stretch into the bridle with a relaxed jaw (figure 51), rather than walk along with nose poked out when he will be both crooked and behind the bit (figure 52).

A driving horse in single harness has his quarters controlled by the shafts. To a lesser degree the horse in long reins can be kept straight by the reins each side of his quarters. The ridden horse can only be kept straight if he obeys an individual leg aid.

In order to understand the requests of an individual leg the horse must be progressively taught to obey such an aid. But first let us imagine what the instinctive reactions of a wild horse would be. Any weight on his back, or straps or rider's legs round his waist, are to his primitive instincts a predatory animal which he fights to get rid of by bucking and bolting. If, by careful handling from birth, the young horse condescends to allow the rider on his back, we still have the problem of teaching him to go forward to driving leg aids applied on the girth and to move his quarters away from a pushing aid applied a hand's breadth behind the same.

By watching a horse in his paddock being tormented by flies in the height of summer we can see what his instinctive reaction is to any irritation on his body. Anything on his quarters is swished off with his tail; anything on his belly he attempts to remove by cow kicking; and an irritation on the shoulders or withers causes him to twitch his muscles. He bites at a fly on his chest, shakes his head at one on his neck, and stamps or paws at the bot fly laying eggs on his forelegs.

Figure 52 *Horse on a long rein, but behind the bit and nose poked out (see Glossary)*

The circus trainer takes advantage of these instincts to train the liberty horse to say "Yes", "No", and 'count', as is the High School horse similarly taught to raise its forelegs in the Spanish Walk or Trot. This is achieved by tickling the horse with the end of the schooling whip at the appropriate place and ceasing immediately the desired reaction is obtained.

From the foregoing observations it is obvious that the required response to the leg aid is contrary to what the horse's instincts tell him to do. For an example: we apply the right leg behind the girth asking the horse to move his quarters from right to left. The green horse thinks this is a fly or some other nuisance which his instincts tell him to get rid of. He swishes his tail, but we continue to ask. Next, he cow-kicks, and, still not getting relief, he side steps to the right hoping to find some post or wall on which to scrape away the irritation.

It is now that we must resort to lateral aids, which are always the remedy for a green or rebellious horse. The right rein, turning the head and neck to the right makes it almost impossible for the horse to do anything other than move his quarters to the left (figure 53). This is a rudimentary turn on the forehand and if the leg aid immediately ceases to ask, the horse is rewarded in the same manner as he is when instinctively removing a fly.

It goes without saying that the further back the leg aids are given, the more likely we are to provoke the horse to cow kick. To apply the legs as close to the girth as possible, the toes must be turned out at an angle of forty five degrees especially when it is necessary to use the spur.

direction of movement

Left leg on the girth, right leg behind the girth. The right rein influences the quarters to move from right to left.

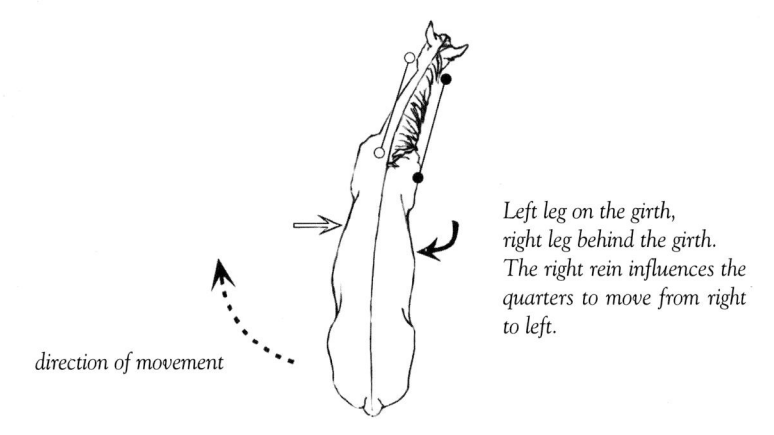

Figure 53 *Lateral aids for obtaining movement of quarters from a green horse*

Contact

As mentioned before, the horse should move freely forward in contact with the reins and no attempt should be made to ask the horse to relax the lower jaw until the rider gets the feeling of restraining the horse rather than having to drive him forward.

Through mishandling, such as standing in the stable or lungeing in over-tight side reins, some youngsters will overbend and refuse to take any contact at all with the bit. Some will even run back violently each time an attempt is made to take up contact. Driving aids, whilst energetic, should be tactful. It is better to put such a horse's quarters into a strong corner where it cannot run back and ask politely with the legs. Sooner or later the horse will take a few steps forward, when the reins should be lightened but not wholly relinquished. The horse will take this as a reward and in time go forward whenever contact is taken up in conjunction with energetic driving aids.

Sometimes the contact is too strong, the horse leaning on the bit to the extent of bruising the tongue and bars of the mouth. Such horses must be schooled for relaxation of the lower jaw without delay. They should be bitted with a thick straight bar snaffle, preferably vulcanite.

Relaxation of the Lower Jaw

The horse will never go freely forward, regardless of how much impulsion is created by the legs, unless the lower jaw is relaxed. In modern times this is referred to as 'submission' but through the history of equitation has been called various names. 'A good mouth' and 'direct flexion' are two other terms which most people are familiar with (see Glossary, page 104). The methods of obtaining submission are as numerous as the names themselves. Likewise, there are many misconceptions of what perfect submission is. I believe that submission through the relaxation of the lower jaw is when the horse champs the bit and immediately swallows its saliva. If there is a froth on the corners of the mouth, the horse is resisting in the lower jaw and submission is incomplete.

Conversely, the horse may open its mouth and cross its lower jaw from side to side. As there is no champing of the bit, the submission is still incomplete. In all cases the horse should be asked to go forward into a restraining rein aid. Because the hands should receive and distribute the impulsion created by the legs, no more impulsion is necessary than the hands can deal with. The leg aids should therefore begin with an almost imperceptible vibration which increases in strength until the desired response has been achieved.

The rider's heels should always be kept deep without being rigid. When the leg aids are about to degenerate into a kick with the toe down, the schooling whip or the spur takes over, first brushing the horse's coat before increasing in severity. In time a positive response will be obtained to the first minute vibration of the calf of the leg, made hard by a reasonably deep but not stiff heel.

Outline

Viewed from the side the horse should carry its head proudly, with its neck flexed at the poll and its face almost perpendicular; the muzzle will be more or less level with a horizontal line from the withers. The back, rounded behind the saddle, will have brought the hind legs under the body, thus attaining balance (figure 54).

Figure 54 *Horse working in correct outline: showing 'rassembler'*

If the head is carried too high, even while the face retains its correct profile, the horse's back will become hollow and its hind legs will be unable to come under the body and fulfil their proper role of propelling the mass forward. The telltale signs as seen from the ground are a straight topline of the neck and a bulge in the gullet (figure 55).

Other more visible evasions are over-bending (figure 56), or getting above the bit and stargazing (figure 58). As with an incomplete submission of the lower jaw, so it is with the evasions of wrong head carriage: energetic requests for forward impulsion into a restraining hand should persist until the desirable outline is achieved. If at this moment the rein aids are lightened and the driving aids are decreased or even temporarily abandoned, the horse will in time take this as a reward and start to move in self carriage.

Needless to say, a perfect outline cannot be given by horses with faulty conformation such as ewe necks or broad jowl bones set so close as to not allow the gullet to fit in-between when flexing. Nevertheless, all horses benefit from intensive schooling to the hand and legs.

Obtaining Submission

Training for submission to the rein aids must take priority over everything else. Forward driving aids are useless if impulsion created by the legs does not go through by the action of a light, submissive mouth. Because of the importance of this some trainers of the past did - and some of the present still do - leave their

Figure 55 *Head too high showing a hollow back, straight topline, and a slight bulge in the gullet. This youngster has escaped the hand and has obtained a reward, as the reins have gone slack.*

youngsters standing in side reins for hours at a time. Using this method is not only inhumane, but is also to work to the rule of the thumb, and to obtain relief the horse either sits in the corner of the loose box and arches his back, or hollows the back and stretches his fore and hind legs out like a rocking horse.

Ultimately, driving a horse in long reins from behind (Chapter 6) is a surer and safer way of obtaining submission as the reins can be instantly dropped whenever

Figure 56 *Overbending*

the youngster gives a negative reaction to the restraining aids. Also, reward can be given immediately after a positive submission by allowing the horse to walk on a long rein.

Some horses which naturally go freely forward will submit to the rein aids at the first attempt to drive them. Others will try every possible evasion before finally surrendering.

It is argued that collection in early stages of training will destroy a youngster's extended paces. This is not the case if the horse is rewarded by lengthening the stride and relaxing the rein aids each and every time it goes into self-carriage. Therefore those horses which go quickly into an outline should be encouraged to go calmly forward, whereas the onward bound youngster that has a strong contact and seeks to go beyond the hand must be held in collection until he calms down. Such horses will often go into an irregular passage or even piaffe before relaxing the lower jaw and going into self carriage.

As mentioned so often in these pages, the whole theory of training is based on opposing what the horse is doing. Thus we lighten the hand to the over-collected horse and encourage him into more extended paces, while the lethargic animal that leans on the bit and refuses to come into outline is driven into extreme collection.

Figure 57 *Horse working in correct outline: this horse is balanced, i.e. in 'ramener' but not yet relaxed enough to be in 'rassembler.' (see figure 54)*

Figure 58 *Above the bit and stargazing, showing hollow back and bulge in gullet*

The Golden Rule

The Golden Rule is to look upon training as a ladder that is climbed a rung at a time. Each lesson is a preparation for the next. If through freshness or lack of work the horse rebels, training should revert to a previous lesson (go back down a rung on the ladder). Should this be met with non-compliance, a still more basic lesson must be tried.

Therefore it is said that lateral aids - leg and rein on the same side - are for a green and rebellious horse, and diagonal aids are for a submissive horse that goes freely forward.

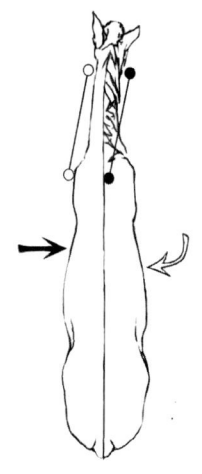

Position
Horse moving forward, left leg on the girth to prevent the horse reining back.
Right leg behind the girth, right rein towards left hip, asking for lateral bend right.

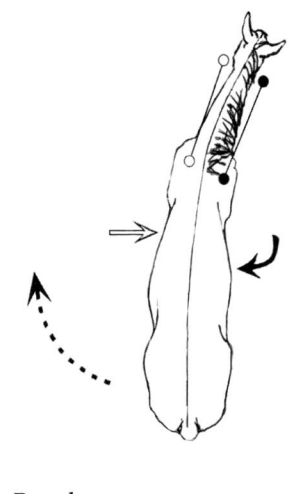

Propel
Horse has now yielded and therefore right rein is now brought back towards the body; as is also the left rein as it needs to be ready to stop the shoulders falling to the left.

Figure 59 *Lateral bend, right leg behind the girth, quarters moving left*

Lateral - sometimes called unilateral - aids are when the rein influences the leg aid on the same side. The most elementary form is the turn on the forehand, which is first carried out on foot when asking the horse to move its quarters across whilst being groomed or mucked out. Young horses handled thus are seldom any trouble when being taught obedience to the leg.

When the horse obeys the request of a leg aid behind the girth and moves its quarters away, the help of the lateral rein (i.e. the rein on the same side) is decreased. These would be described as direct aids. In time the opposite rein to the leg is applied which would be the use of diagonal aids.

The rider must feel the ideas of the horse (equestrian tact) and act accordingly. There is nothing to compare with the old adage 'position and propel'; for example, getting the horse to yield his head and neck to the right before applying the right

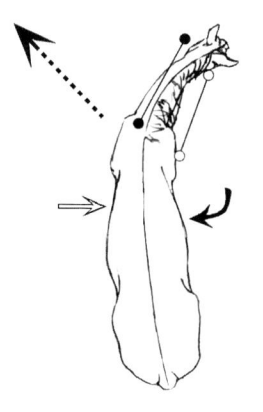

Horse overbending to the right.
Forehand escaping to the left instead of quarters moving to the left.

To correct: Active right leg behind the girth sends impulsion into restraining left hand.
Right hand being 'polite'.
Both hands carried to the right to counter shoulders falling to the left.

Figure 60 *Accentuated bend to right, forehand to left*

leg behind the girth to ask the quarters to move to the left (lateral effects). Should the horse refuse to yield to the right rein, the left leg on the girth should drive the horse forward until it submits and bends laterally to the right, when the right leg behind the girth once more asks the quarters to move to the left (figure 59).

Alternatively, the horse may volunteer an accentuated bend to the right rein and, instead of moving its quarters away from the right leg, take its forehand across to the left (figure 60). In this case, the left rein in stronger contact will control the bend of the neck. Needless to say, in all these exercises the horse should gain a little ground in a forward direction. To perform them stationary is to run the risk of allowing the horse to rein back.

Conversely, in the case of a horse that does not understand how to rein back, a turn on the forehand from halt is a good preparation (the previous rung of the ladder).

Half-halts

A half-halt is usually a reduction of pace or tempo within the gait the horse is in at that particular time. It should be used either to re-establish rhythm or shorten a stride and collect a horse in preparation for a smooth transition up or down to another gait.

The word 'pace' is often used to mean walk, trot or canter, which would more properly be described as 'gaits'. In fact, pace is the time taken in minutes to cover a certain number of metres. Tempo is the rate of foot falls per minute. Rhythm is the regularity of foot falls within a particular gait, (that is, for example, an even two time in trot, or four time in walk), the tempo of a rhythm being mainly dictated by the length of the horse's legs. Thus, for the same pace, the tempo of a pony in rhythm in any particular gait is much faster than that of a 16.2 hands horse in the same gait. It is possible to get a variation of tempo whilst still maintaining an even rhythm, this variation being necessary at the beginning of schooling for the lengthening and shortening of strides.

The three gaits of a riding horse are walk, trot and canter. Anything faster than an extended canter is a gallop, when the sequence of foot falls is inevitably irregular. From the foregoing remarks it will be seen that the horse with a quick tempo can go at a fast pace but be 'beyond' rhythm (i.e. have irregular footfalls). In correct equitation, increase or decrease of pace within a specific gait should be obtained by lengthening and shortening the stride within the rhythm.

The half-halt is obtained by the horse bending itself longitudinally (in direct flexion). Thus, as the rider's leg aids send the impulsion to the restraining rein aids, the schooled horse brings its hindquarters further under its body, whilst at the same time relaxing its lower jaw and flexing at the poll.

The foregoing aids are all that are necessary for a schooled horse especially if he has been accustomed to and is wearing a double bridle. However, many problems are met with when the tyro trainer is schooling in the orthodox way with a jointed snaffle.

As the nutcracker action of the jointed snaffle must be very uncomfortable, the trained horse should relax its lower jaw and volunteer a direct flexion to obtain the reward of comfort. However, as the green horse usually tries other ways of gaining comfort, it leans on one rein only, thus bringing the bit through that side of its mouth with the joint more or less resting on the bar of the mouth. Whilst not giving complete comfort the horse apparently finds it more comfortable than the nutcracker action and it begins to become one-sided or crooked.

If the incompetent rider attempts to reduce pace by pulling a little harder (figure 61b), the horse will veer to the side he resists on. The tyro rider will then haul on the opposite rein hoping to bring the horse back to track. Should the rein on the resisting side still be held, this would bring the bit back into the correct

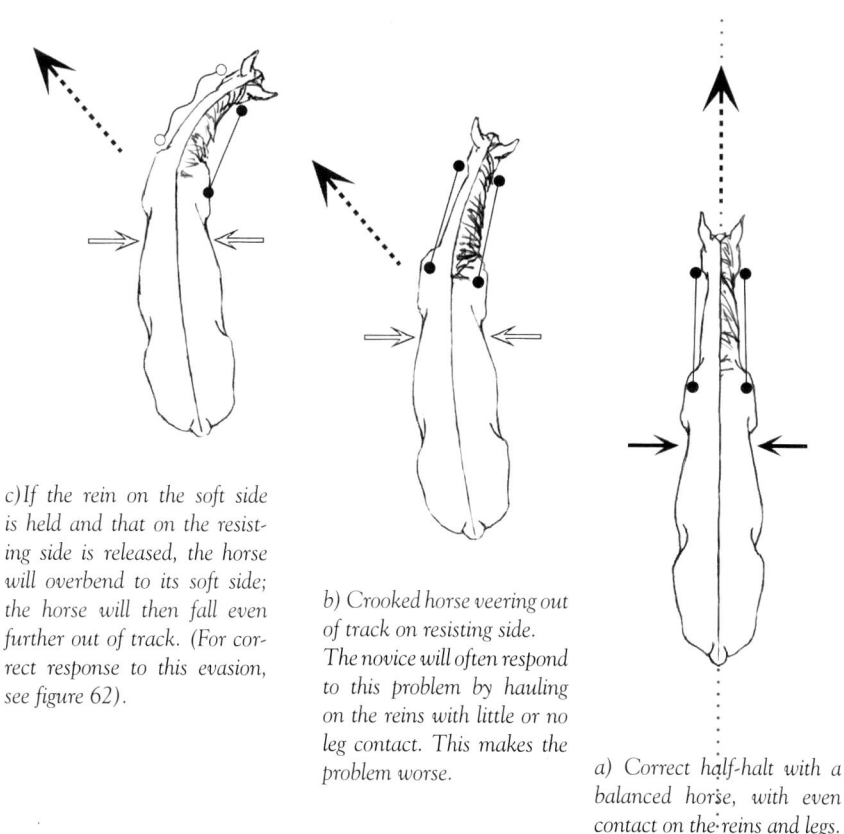

c) If the rein on the soft side is held and that on the resisting side is released, the horse will overbend to its soft side; the horse will then fall even further out of track. (For correct response to this evasion, see figure 62).

b) Crooked horse veering out of track on resisting side. The novice will often respond to this problem by hauling on the reins with little or no leg contact. This makes the problem worse.

a) Correct half-halt with a balanced horse, with even contact on the reins and legs.

Figure 61 Crooked horse falling out of track

position and the nutcracker action would persuade the horse to seek comfort by stopping. Although this is a reliable method of stopping a horse that is making off and increasing pace, it should only be done in an emergency as the half-halt or full halt is then incorrectly made on the forehand. This would ultimately lead to a horse coming behind the bit.

Conversely, if the novice rider hauls on the soft or unresisting rein and at the same time releases the contact on the resisting side, the horse will overbend at the withers, thus loading the shoulder on that side and producing a shorter stride. This in turn would make for a further falling out of track rather than bringing the horse back onto it (figure 61c). Therefore the horse must be corrected of any tendency to become crooked before it can be asked to execute a proper half-halt.

Straightening the Crooked Horse

To correct crookedness and maintain straightness the rider should always try to keep the horse on the track which he - the rider - imagines his mount should follow. Whether this is riding one of the school figures within the menage, keeping a certain distance from the verge on a quiet country lane, or trying to keep a straight line whilst going across open fields, the aims are always the same.

The horse has always a tendency to veer off to the side on which he takes the strongest contact, here the left. In that case, to bring him back to track, the rider should carry both hands to the right, maintaining a contact with the resisting side - the left - and being polite with the right hand (figure 62a). As mentioned before, this would stop the horse on its forehand, so it is imperative that the right leg on the girth keeps the horse moving forward. If the horse does not then return to the track on its right, the right leg should move back a hand's breadth to the position behind the girth (figure 62b); the horse will then move its quarters from right to left, thus doing a turn on the forehand to the right.

As the horse approaches the track, the hands are still carried to the right, but now the right leg moves forward onto the girth. This sends the impulsion onto the left rein which asks the horse to bend to the left. The left leg is now moved a hand's breadth behind the girth as a pushing aid (figure 62c), and the horse will leg-yield back to track (figure 62d).

Although this is incorrect equitation and if practised too often would result in the horse getting behind the bit, in the case of a novice rider and a green horse it succeeds in getting the horse to change direction to the right. I would defend any criticism for advocating this method by claiming that lateral aids should always be used on a green or rebellious horse. Diagonal aids are only effective when the impulsion created by an individual leg is received and distributed by the opposite rein. Thus, a turn on the forehand, being lateral equitation, is a preparation for a turn on the haunches, which is diagonal equitation.

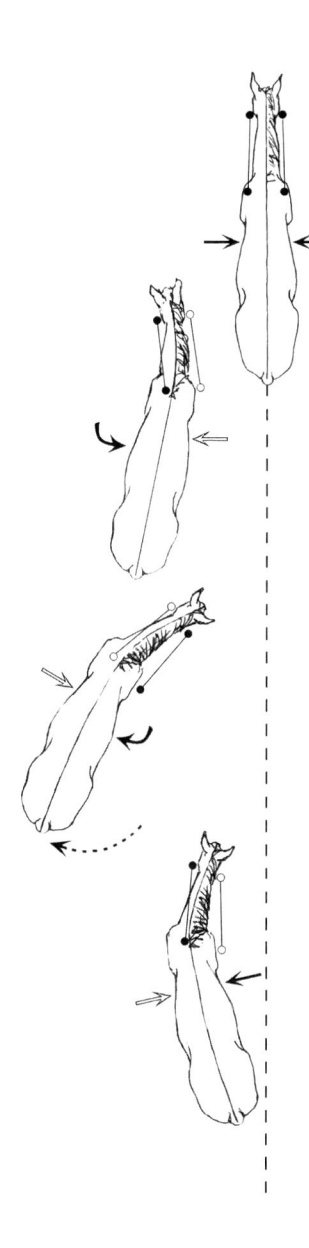

d) Here the horse has changed direction to the right, moved his quarters from right to left, and returned to track. The hands are once again carried straight.

c) Only when the horse moves forward can the right leg move back onto the girth. The left rein now asks for left bend, and the energetic left leg, now behind the girth on the hollow left side causes the horse to leg-yield back to track.

b) If the horse does not return to track, (the resisting outside rein may cause the nappy horse to stop) the right leg should move back a hand's breadth to the postion behind the girth. This is still the active leg - it sends impulsion to the shoulders and keeps the horse moving forwards.

Both hands should still be carried as in a), but the right rein should now be the dominant one. The left rein should, however, oppose any further movement to the left by the shoulders.

The quarters should then move to the left to face the horse back in the direction of the track.

a) Crooked horse falling out of track and also behind the bit.

To correct this evasion, carry both hands to right maintaining contact on the resisting (here the left) side and being 'polite'with right hand (soft side).

The active right leg on the girth keeps the horse moving forward.

Figure 62 Bringing the crooked horse back to track

73

Chapter Eight
Thoughts on Schooling
Part 2 : Lateral Movements, Canter Leads, and Particular Problems Illustrated

Side-Steps or Lateral Movements

It is better to put the young horse through intensive training in lateral work before canter is asked for. More than any other gait, is it essential that the adage of 'position and propel' be applied to canter. Since canter work puts extra strain on the legs, lateral movements in their various guises are excellent preparation for canter without running the risk of hammering the legs.

Horse's head looking to right.

Horse pivots about the right foreleg and left fore steps round it.

Rider's left leg on the girth, right leg behind the girth.

Quarters move from right to left with right hindleg stepping under the body and in front of left hindleg.

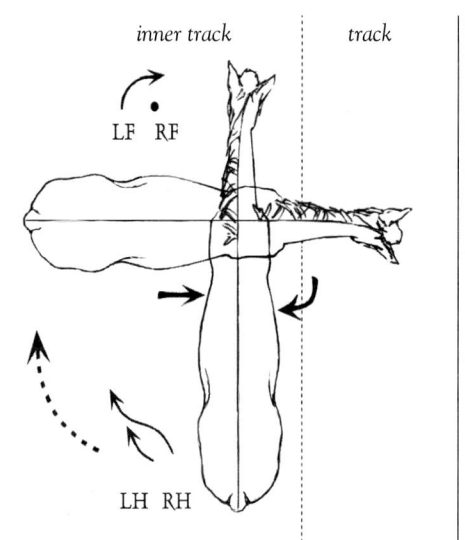

Figure 63 *Turn on the forehand to the right*

Adhering to the principle of climbing the ladder a rung at a time, those movements requiring lateral equitation are first practised, and as the horse becomes obedient to the leg, the more difficult exercises are done.

As mentioned before, the turn on the forehand (figure 63) has been used in a rudimentary way to point the green horse that was not going forward in the right

74

Head straight or slightly turned to the right.

Horse pivots about the left hindleg and right foreleg steps in front of left foreleg.

Rider's left leg on the girth, right leg behind the girth.

In an elementary turn on the haunches to the left, the head turned away from the direction of movement frees the left shoulder.

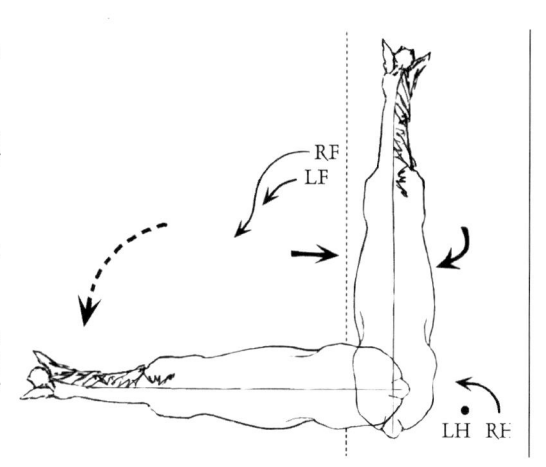

Figure 64 Turn on the haunches to the left (Elementary Only)

direction. It has also been seen that the horse that overbends (say to the right) as an evasion, takes his forehand to the left, which is a turn on the haunches (figure 64). By getting the forehand and the quarters to move to the left simultaneously,

The horse's head and neck are bent slightly away from direction of movement in order to free the left shoulder.

Both fore and hind right legs step in front and across left fore and hind ones.

The horse's body is parallel to the long side of the school.

Rider's left leg on the girth, right leg behind the girth.

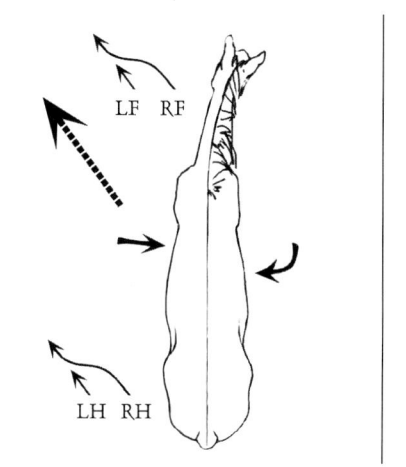

Figure 65 Leg-yield to the left

we have succeeded in getting the horse to leg-yield (figure 65). The head turned away from the direction in which the horse is moving frees the left shoulder allowing it to go to the left, whilst at the same time the turn of the head is helping the right leg behind the girth move the quarters to the left.

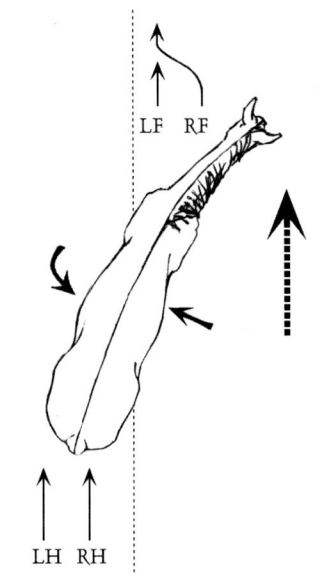

Forehand on inside track, right foreleg crossing in front of its partner.

Hindquarters moving straight along the track.

Rider's right leg on the girth, left leg behind the girth.

Horse bent round rider's inside leg.

Figure 66 Right shoulder-in

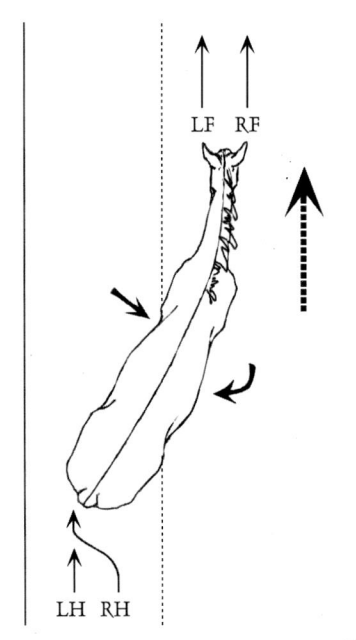

Forehand on inside track, moving fairly straight.

Hinquarters on outside track.

Inside hindleg stepping under body and in front of its outside partner.

Rider's left leg on the girth, right leg behind the girth.

Figure 67 Renvers

The tail-to-the-wall movements of shoulder-in (figure 66) and renvers (figure 67) both require the horse to respond to diagonal aids, although in shoulder-in the horse is looking in the opposite direction to which he is going, whereas in renvers he is looking in the same direction he is going.

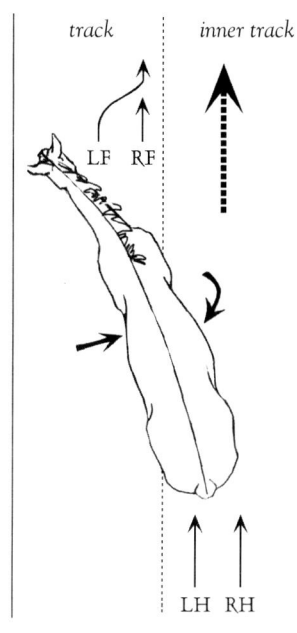

Forehand on track, outside foreleg crossing in front of inside one.

Hindquarters on inside track, moving fairly straight.

Rider's left leg on the girth, right leg behind the girth.

Horse bent round rider's outside leg.

Figure 68 *Right shoulder-out*

For shoulder-in to the right, the left leg behind the girth prevents the quarters from shaving the wall whilst the right leg on the girth maintains impulsion. The forehand is bent round the rider's inside leg and moves more laterally than the quarters which should move more or less straight along the outside track. In renvers to the right, the left leg on the girth maintains impulsion and the right leg behind the girth pushes the quarters to the left. The quarters are bent round the rider's left leg and move laterally whereas the forehand on the inside track moves more or less straight.

The same explanations apply to the exercises of head to the wall, - namely shoulder-out (figure 68) and travers (figure 69).

Finally the horse will execute half-pass (figure 70), moving laterally along an incline and looking in the direction it is going (diagonal equitation).

LF RF

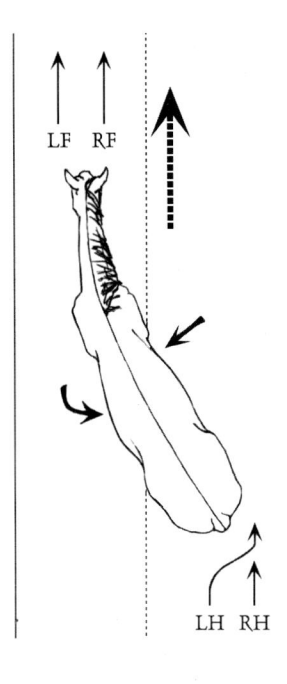

LH RH

Forehand on outside track, moving fairly straight, and hindquarters on inside track.

Horse's outside hind leg steps across and in front of its inside partner.

Rider's right leg on the girth, left leg behind the girth.

Figure 69 *Travers*

All lateral exercises will supple the horse in the whole of its body enabling the rider to keep it straight down the centre line etc. and curved appropriately on bends. Moreover the work gives the rider 'feel' in noticing when the horse is escaping the rein aids or disobeying the leg.

If, for an example, the horse moving in either half-pass or leg-yielding to the left escapes the hand by taking his shoulders too quickly to the left, the rider should counter this by carrying both hands to the right. This puts a stronger pressure on the left rein, thereby bending the head and neck to the left and loading the shoulder on that side. In turn, this will shorten the stride of the left leg, giving the quarters chance to catch up, provided the right leg behind the girth continues to push.

Alternatively, if the quarters move to the side faster than the forehand the hands should be carried to the left with a stronger pressure on the right rein. This will bend the neck slightly to the right, freeing the left shoulder and enabling it to gain ground to the left. The left leg on the girth maintains impulsion.

The first priority is to keep the horse between the hand and the leg. As he becomes more supple and obedient the head and neck can be placed wherever the rider wants.

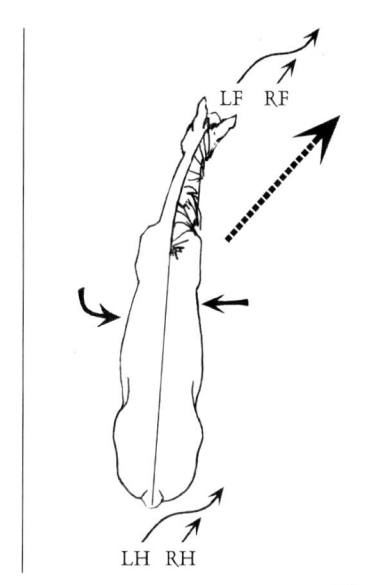

The horse's head looks in the direction of movement.

Fore and hind left legs step in front of and across the right hand pair.

Rider's right leg on the girth, left leg behind the girth.

(This is more difficult than leg-yielding as the lateral bend to the right cramps the freedom of the right shoulder.)

Figure 70 *Half-pass*

Obtaining Correct Canter Lead

To obtain a correct canter lead when working on a straight line, it is essential that the rider is able to 'position and propel'. The more lateral suppleness the horse has acquired at work in trot, the easier it will be to get the correct canter lead at the first time of asking.

Natural crookedness in the horse will remain with it until its life's end. Therefore the rider must apply the aids in a rational rather than a rigid and methodical manner in order to counter the one-sidedness which the horse continually adopts to evade the more difficult exercises the rider asks for.

Although the rein aids are carried to one side or the other to ask the forehand to change direction, or to counter the same as the horse tries to evade the hand, the strongest contact must always be on the side which the horse resists. Likewise, the leg a hand's breadth behind the girth asks the quarters to move away and a leg on the girth asks the horse to go forward; but only one leg acts energetically: namely, the leg on the side to which the horse is incurved (i.e. the horse's soft side).

In all these pages it is assumed that the horse resists on the left and overbends to the right; so when it is asked for a canter to the left it will do so easily as its left shoulder is free, although the head and neck, bent to the right, will earn poor marks in a dressage test for wrong lateral bend. However, when the cavalry were in urgent need of more horses this was found to be the most expedient way to obtain a canter on a named leg with a green horse.

Just as leg-yielding precedes the half-pass on the rungs of the training ladder, so is the canter strike off with a wrong lateral bend (sometimes called 'inside out') a preparation for the more sophisticated canter with the horse slightly flexed at the poll in the direction in which it is moving.

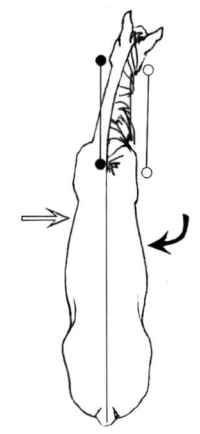

The rider's energetic right leg is behind the girth, and the passive left leg is on the girth. Rein contact is maintained with the resisting side, with an open rein on the soft (here right) side 'thumbing a lift'.

Figure 71 *Aids for canter on stiff (here left) side*

To obtain a correct strike off to the left, the horse should first be positioned to the left with an outside leg aid sending the impulsion onto the inside rein, thus asking for a bend around the rider's passive inside leg. When this is achieved, an energetic inside leg aid propels the impulsion onto the outside hand and the horse strikes into canter correctly.

The green youngster may confuse the leg aid on the girth with the one behind - there being only a hand's breadth difference - and instead of striking off in canter, turn his head back to the right, putting himself in shoulder-out position and escaping the hand by rushing off in trot.

An outside leg aid behind the girth must now ask once more for a position to the left, and carrying both hands to the right will slightly free the left shoulder (see figure 71). If a canter on the left lead is obtained it will have been by the old fashioned English aids of an energetic outside leg aid. This is better than no canter at all and the reins should give a little to reward the youngster for its efforts.

With the one-sided horse who is stiff on the left, on asking for canter to the right the problems are entirely different. Since the horse has a tendency to overbend to the right, positioning is superfluous and all that is needed is to propel the horse with an energetic inside leg aid into canter. However, instead of turning its head and neck slightly to the left when the outside rein receives the impulsion created by the right leg, the youngster may mistake this driving aid on the girth for a pushing aid behind the girth and throw its quarters to the left, striking off into false canter (figure 72a).

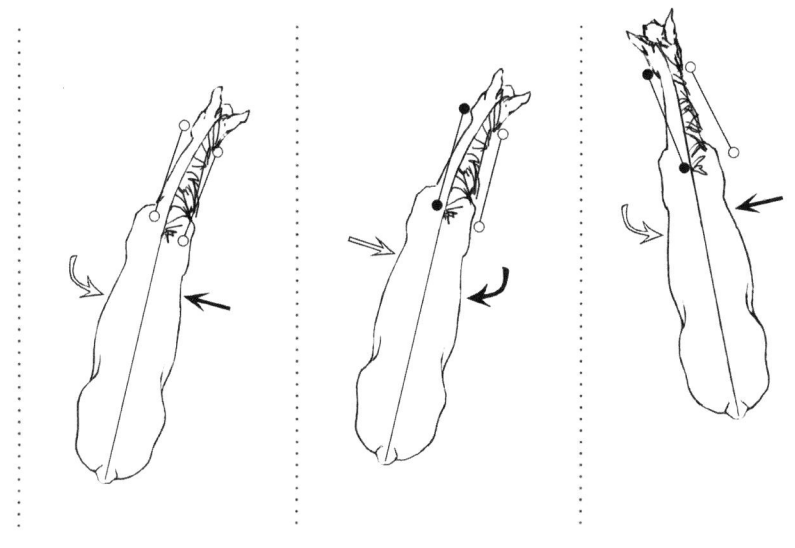

a) Orthodox aids have been applied. An energetic inside leg on the girth has created impulsion but the horse is overloading his right shoulder and has moved his quarters to the left.

b) To correct, the rider's right leg moves behind the girth, and asks for left bend.

c) In response the horse has adopted a shoulder-out position. The inside leg can now be applied energetically on the girth. The canter obtained should be on the correct lead (though on the wrong bend).

Figure 72 Aids for canter right in a horse soft on the right side

The rider should continue to use the right leg energetically, but now move it to a position behind the girth and ask the horse to bend to the left (figure 72a). These aids will bring the horse politely into trot and by now carrying both hands to the right the horse will adopt the position of shoulder-out. The inside leg is once more brought forward and applied energetically on the girth (figure 72c), when the horse will strike off with the correct canter lead - albeit with wrong lateral bend.

As the youngster with the one-sided mouth becomes submissive and supple to the rein on the stiff (here the left) side, it may use shoulder-out as an evasion to rush out in trot.

As previously mentioned in canter to the left, the outside leg and inside rein carried towards the rider's left hip counter this evasion and ask the horse for correct canter to the right. As before, in the unlikely event of the horse striking off to the old fashioned English aids, it should not be punished, but allowed to canter on.

It will have been noted that, in canter to the left, an energetic right leg behind the girth sends the impulsion onto the left rein whilst the hands carried to the right deter the horse from side-stepping to the left. In canter to the right, once again it is the energetic right leg aid (this time on the girth) that sends the impulse onto the left rein. The hands are as before carried to the right, this time to encourage the horse to move in right shoulder-out.

Therefore, in requesting either canter lead on a horse that resists on the left rein, the right leg is the most energetic; similarly, in each case the hands are carried to the right. Only the position of the leg aids are different.

Needless to say, all the above aids are reversed for horses that resist on the right rein, and are soft on or overbend to the left.

Frequent stops and starts at canter make the horse listen to its rider's aids and become very responsive. It is then that another rung of the ladder is climbed and correct position in canter is asked for. With a daily improvement in lateral suppleness the horse can then be correctly positioned and then propelled into canter by the orthodox aids of inside leg and outside rein.

Problems Caused by a One-Sided Mouth: Working in Circles

All the examples below are for a horse stiff on the left rein, and overbent on the right rein. Reverse all these solutions to correct the movements of the horse who is soft on the right rein.

Solution
Active inside (right) leg on the girth asks horse to go forward into restraining outside rein.
Inside (right) rein in open position.

b) Horse brought back to track

Problem
Horse over-bending at withers to right no relaxation of lower jaw and falling out through the shoulder.

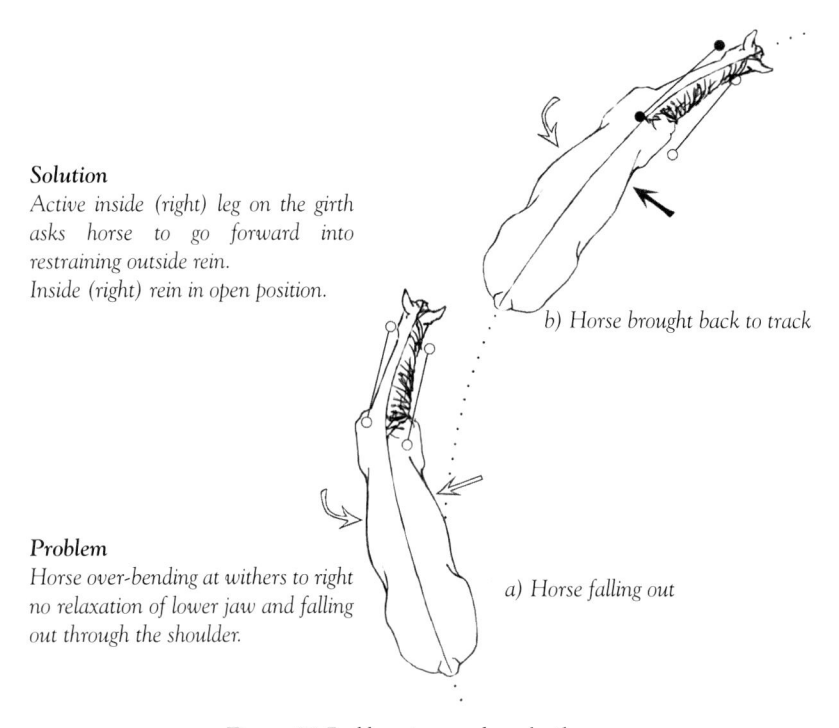

a) Horse falling out

Figure 73 *Problems in trot, the soft side*

Problem: in trot on right rein the horse (who is soft on the right) is overbending at the withers and will show no relaxation of lower jaw, thus causing shoulders to fall out (figure 73a).

Solution: 'thumb a lift' (open rein) to inside with little or no contact. The rider's inside leg (hollow side) on the girth should then ask the horse to go forward into a restraining outside rein. When the horse volunteers to submit to this request and takes its head and neck to the left, the shoulders will move to the left and back on to the track (figure 73b).

Problem: in trot on left rein; overbending at withers to outside and no relaxation of lower jaw, thus causing shoulders to fall in (figure 74a).

Solution: 'thumb a lift' (open rein) to outside with little or no contact. The rider's outside leg (hollow side) behind the girth asks the horse to carry his quarters to the left, and also asks for impulsion which will be received on the restraining inside rein. The inside hand is carried towards the rider's outside hip, which asks the horse to take its shoulders out and bend its head inwards (figure 74b). When the horse has yielded to these requests it is correctly bent round a passive inside leg.

Solution

Dominant outside (right) leg behind the girth, restraining inside (left) rein with inside hand carried towards rider's outside (right) hip.

b) Horse moved back to track

Problem

Overbending at withers to outside, and shoulders falling in.

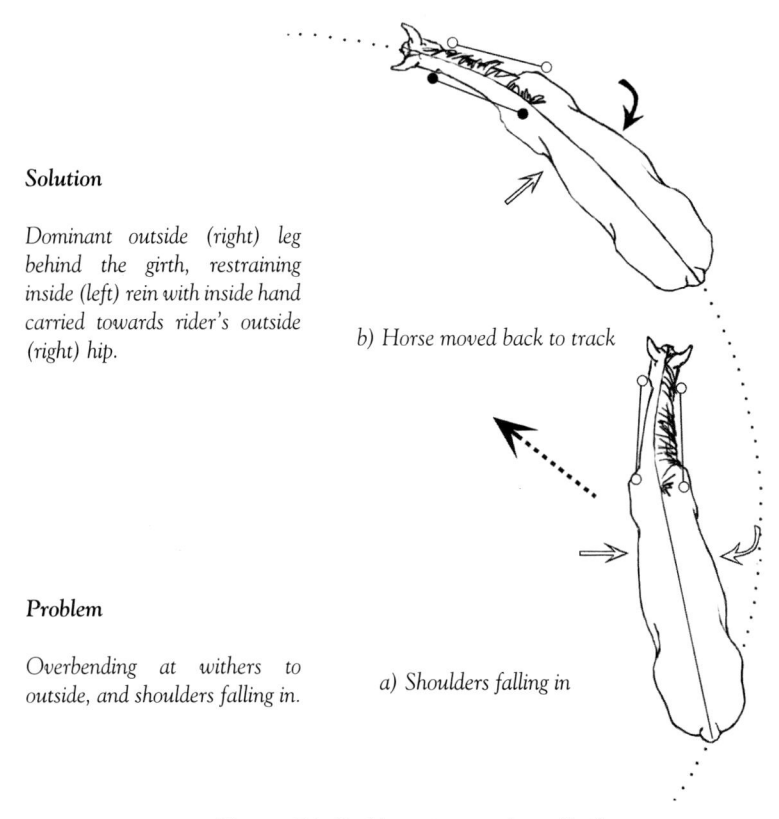

a) Shoulders falling in

Figure 74 *Problems in trot, the stiff side*

Ideally, the contact should now be on the outside rein, with inside leg maintaining impulsion; but a confirmed one-sided horse, through muscular fatigue, will quickly revert to its old habits. Therefore every horse, from day one of his schooling, should be ridden sixty seconds to the minute. A long rein walk is the best reward for obedience.

Problem: In canter to right, quarters out and neck overbent inwards at the withers. The horse is in a crude position of shoulder-in and it is therefore impossible to canter except on the wrong leg, which it should not do if it is being faithful to the aids, as the outside leg is behind, and the inside leg on, the girth (figure 75a).

Incidentally, this is an elementary position to obtain counter-canter if the leg aids are reversed: viz.-outside leg on, and inside leg behind, the girth.

c) Energetic inside leg creates impulsion which is received on the left rein.
The horse's head and neck bend slightly to the left freeing the right shoulder. The horse will now be a bit 'shoulder-out'. He should now canter on the correct lead, albeit with the wrong bend.

b) Carrying both hands to the right, energetic outside leg behind the girth, putting horse in travers position. The right leg should be passive and still .

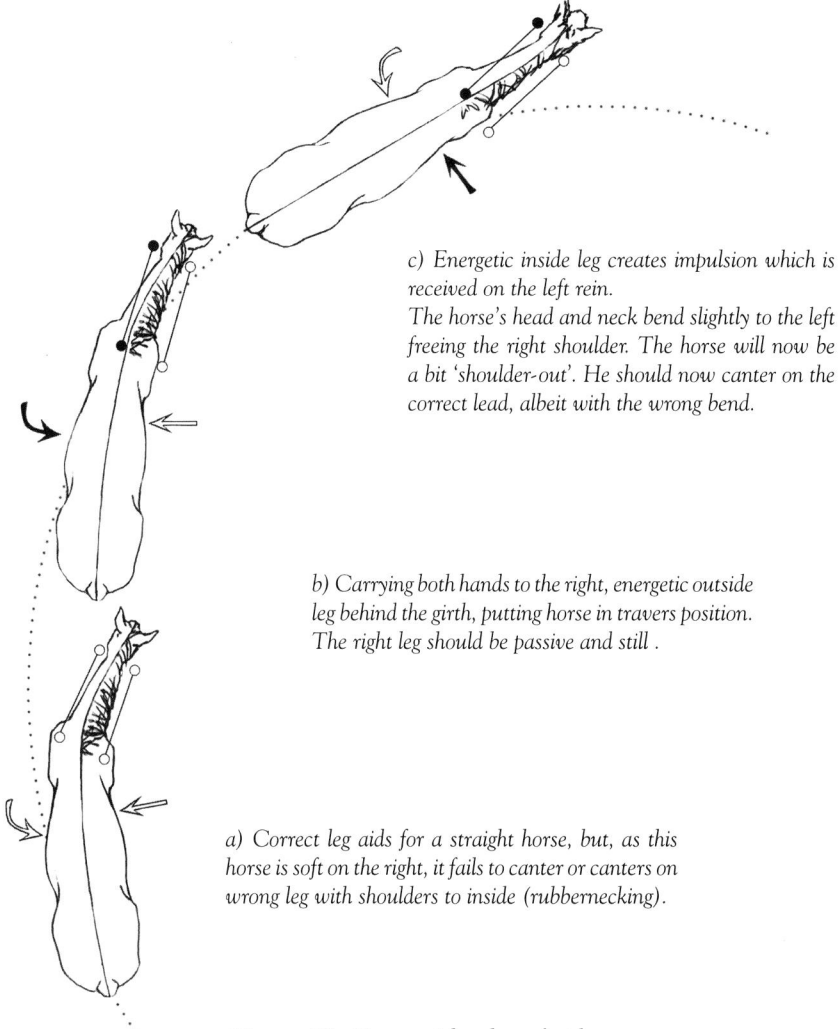

a) Correct leg aids for a straight horse, but, as this horse is soft on the right, it fails to canter or canters on wrong leg with shoulders to inside (rubbernecking).

Figure 75 Canter right, the soft side

Solution: First carry both hands to the right and use an energetic outside leg behind the girth (figure 75b). This puts the horse in travers position (figure 69.) As its quarters are now carried inwards, it can do no other than canter with the correct (inside) leg, but would find it difficult as the inside (leading) shoulder is overloaded. The right (inside) rein thumbs a lift, with little or no contact, whilst an energetic inside leg (hollow side) on the girth creates impulsion, which is received on the left rein (figure 75c). The submissive and supple horse will then slightly bend its head and neck to the left, thus freeing the right shoulder and loading the left. If sufficient impulsion is volunteered by the horse a correct canter is a certainty.

WARNING: Continual and excessive schooling at canter can cause damage to the limbs; tendons and muscles being strained when there is deep going or when the ground is slippy, and joints being concussed when the ground is rock hard. Lateral suppling exercises - i.e. correctly ridden serpentines and circles for a horse not going freely forward, and sidesteps in some form for an onward bound horse - are best done in a slow rhythm at trot. In the case of the equine subject of this treatise, most leg-yields are practised from left to right; and when riding circles, left shoulder-in when going anticlockwise and right shoulder-out when going clockwise.

More Problems in Canter on Circles: Napping Out and Spiralling In

Problem: Sometimes the horse naps to the left, in the direction of the stable or its companions, instead of continuing freely forward on a right hand circle. It does this by taking a firm hold of the left rein and turning its head to the right. This immediately over-loads the shoulder of the leading leg and destroys canter (figure 76a). Conversely, it may grab the right rein and threaten to rear. As the rider is obliged to let go the contact in case the horse should topple over backwards the horse is rewarded for this and will rear every time it wants to go home.

Solution: Ride with little or no contact on the right rein and as the horse veers to the left move the right leg back a hand's breadth behind the girth, driving the horse forward onto a left hand circle (figure 76b). On arrival back to track, carry both hands to the right to move on a right hand circle and move the inside leg forward onto the girth (figure 76c). If the evasion is repeatedly opposed in this way the horse will submit and commence to go forward whilst maintaining a light contact. The canter to the right can then be asked for again.

N.B. On the small left hand circle continue to carry both hands to the right - the hollow side - the left rein carried towards the right hip. When the horse submits in the lower jaw, it will bend to the left and be free in the right shoulder as it hits the right hand track.

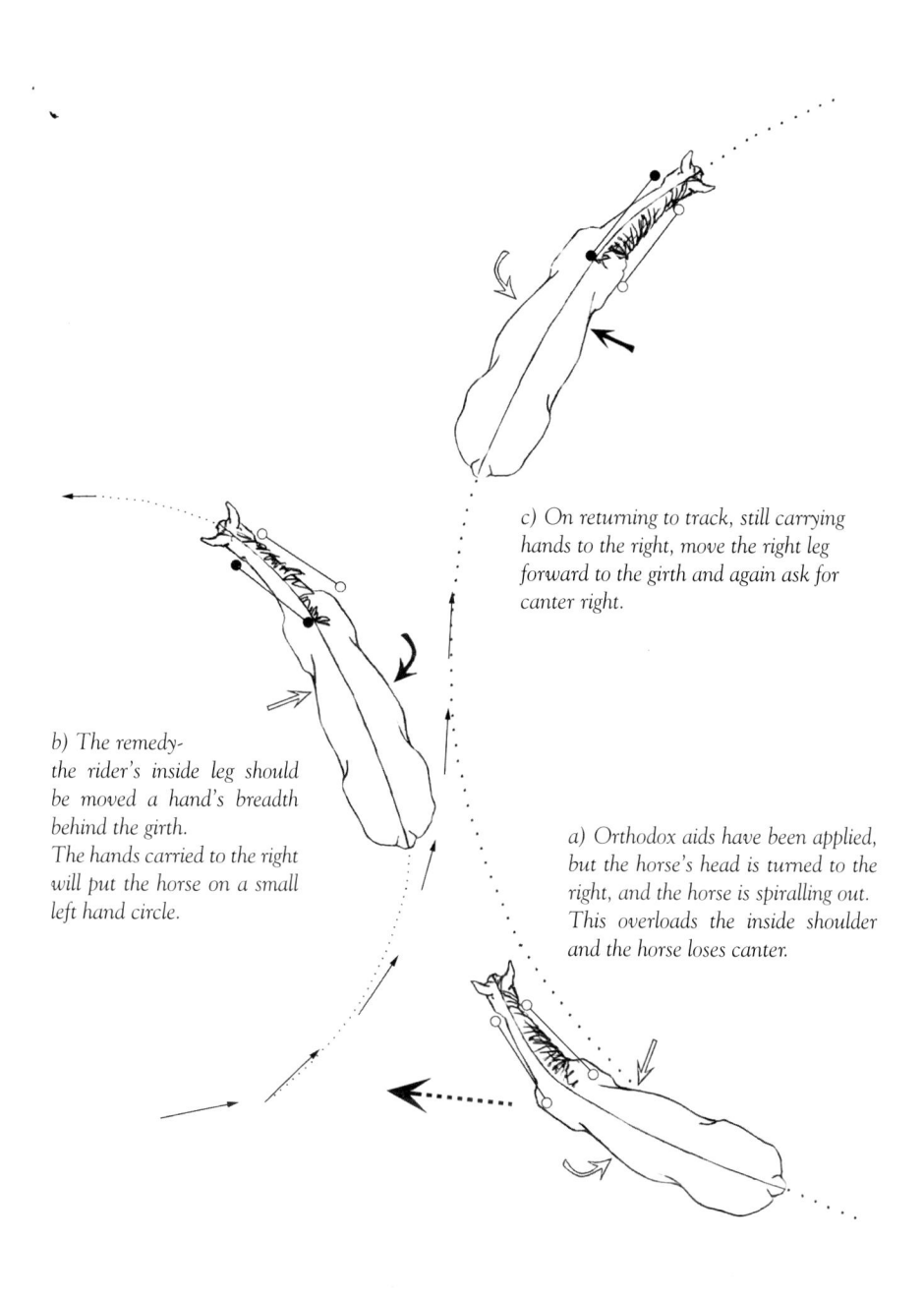

c) On returning to track, still carrying hands to the right, move the right leg forward to the girth and again ask for canter right.

b) The remedy-
the rider's inside leg should be moved a hand's breadth behind the girth.
The hands carried to the right will put the horse on a small left hand circle.

a) Orthodox aids have been applied, but the horse's head is turned to the right, and the horse is spiralling out. This overloads the inside shoulder and the horse loses canter.

Figure 76 *Horse napping to the outside of the circle (falling out through the shoulder)*

87

b) An energetic outside (right) leg creates impulsion on the hollow side which is received by a restraining inside hand, and the horse returns to track.

a) Horse spiralling in (or 'falling in').

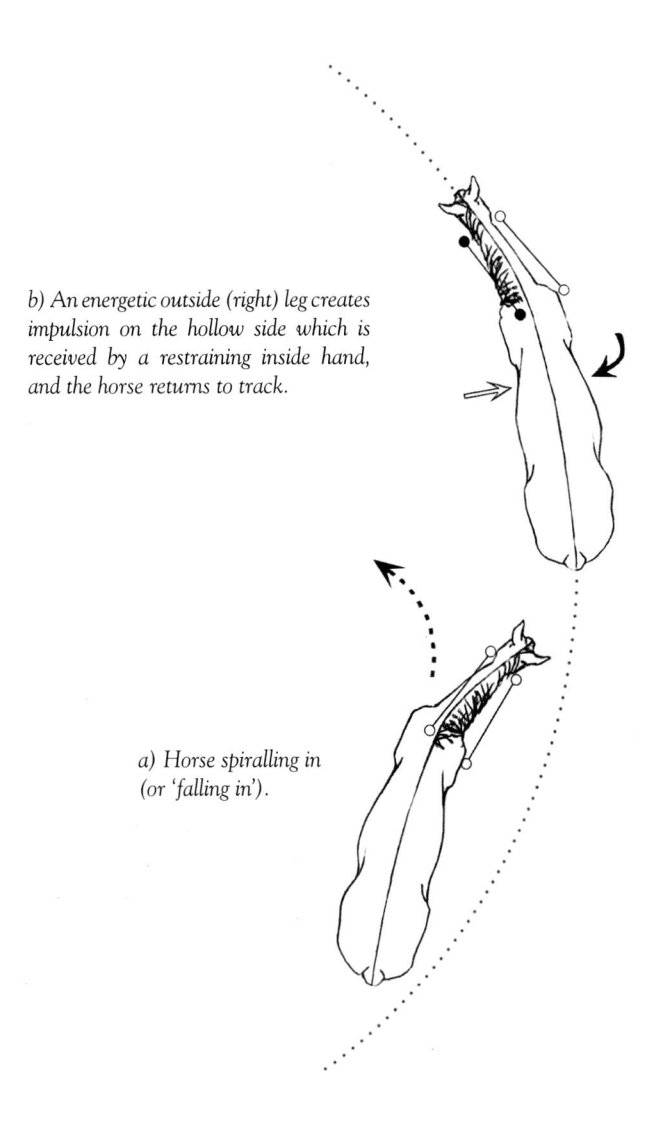

Figure 77 *Horse spiralling in when cantering in a circle on the stiff side (falling in)*

Problem: Because the horse which is the subject of this treatise is stiff on the left rein (hollow on the right), the left shoulder is free and the left canter lead (albeit inside out) is easily obtained. However, the shoulders can move too freely to the left, thus spiralling in and making the circle smaller and smaller (figure 77a).

Solution: As the quarters are always carried slightly to the inside in canter, the only way to get back to the larger circle is by doing a rudimentary counter-canter, i.e., carry both hands to the right to stop the forehand escaping too quickly to the left and energetically attack with the outside leg (the hollow side) to persuade the quarters to take a longer stride to the left (figure 77b). If, on arriving at track, the horse tries to nap for home, carrying both hands to the left will probably succeed in sending it on the anticlockwise circle.

The previous pages are based on the assumption that no horse is perfectly straight, and that it will use its natural crookedness to escape the rider's request to come into outline. Unlike a mechanically propelled vehicle, which can be guided by a touch of the steering wheel and foot pedal, an equine has a mind of its own and will always take the easy option if allowed to do so.

By experience, the trainer should acquire what is known as 'equestrian tact' or 'feel', whereby they sense what the horse is doing at the present moment and also anticipate the evasions it is about to make. As previously mentioned, the trainer cannot physically force the horse to do something, but if he patiently opposes its evasions the horse will eventually go forward in obedience to the aids.

In some of the diagrams, where a leg or rein aid should be dominant, it is shown in stronger black. It will be seen that the dominant leg is usually on the soft (here the right) side. If the horse resists on one rein, it is the opposite leg which creates impulsion, regardless of whether it is inside leg into outside hand or vice-versa. This is referred to as rational as opposed to methodical equitation, methodical equitation being the use of aids that are applied in the orthodox manner, no matter how crooked the horse may be.

A good guide is to apply the leg aid on the side to which the horse 'shows an eye' and also to carry the reins to that side.

Chapter Nine
Thoughts on Jumping

Wild horses only jump an obstacle when the sheer speed of flight prevents them from going round it. Likewise foals and young horses at play in pasture will skip over a bunch of thistles or fallen branch that is in their path. This is probably

Figure 78 *Young horse jumping small obstacle from trot*

Mother Nature's way of practising the youngster's skills at jumping against the day when it flees from a predator. With the odd exception most mature horses do not jump unless obliged to do so and even where the grass is greener on the other side of the fence they do not jump over unless it is very low. Therefore it is logical to assume that any jumping a horse does whilst carrying a rider is the result of training.

Figure 79a, b *Approaching the jump in canter showing the horse lowering head and neck on approach*

Figure 79c, d, e *Jumping in an elongated canter stride*

In the first instance a jump to the horse is merely an obstacle it must negotiate in the same way it steps over or passes any object it meets when being ridden on the flat. Therefore initial training is to ride the horse over a variety of small obstacles in trot (figure 78). These will be stepped or hopped over according to their height As the young horse confidently goes over these small obstacles in response to the rider's co-ordinated aids, it can be cantered at them. If lengthening and shortening of stride have been practised in the menage, the rider can now assist the horse to go over the obstacle more or less in an elongated canter stride (see figure 79).

Likewise, the schooling for counter-canter now becomes of practical use. For example, the young horse cantering towards the obstacle with the near fore leading will invariably try to run out to the left. He can be brought back over the centre of the jump by riding left counter-canter.

Figure 80 Jumping with a fluent arc: the parabola

Quite often the unthinking rider - concerned only with getting the horse over the jump at any price - will unconsciously force the horse to change legs or even trot at the very moment when the maximum impetus is required to launch the horse and rider over the obstacle. The horse may also change legs as it jumps, if the rider inadvertently alters rein and leg aids on the take-off stride.

It is logical to conclude that on showjumping courses where a change of direction followed by a jump comes quickly after a landing over the previous one, there will be problems if the horse lands with the wrong leg leading. In these cases the rider has no option but to ask for a flying change or simple change of lead through trot according to the horse's stage of training.

Scores of excellent books and articles have been published setting out the relative distances for trotting poles and cavalletti whereby a horse is prepared for jumping (figure 78). It is important that the distances suit the individual horse's stride so that it jumps in a fluent arc, sometimes referred to as the parabola (figure 80). An assistant is necessary to adjust the trotting poles to their correct distances (figure 81). Once adjusted, if every other pole were to be removed they would be at the correct distances for canter strides (figure 82). In the absence of any assistance the poles can be laid out in a circle and by increasing and decreasing the radius of the circle ridden, the rider can find the right track for their particular horse.

Cavalletti are not suitable for use in the same way as trotting poles, but a row of them placed a canter stride apart makes the young horse agile and will encourage him to look where he is going. For the youngster that rushes his fences, cavalletti can be placed at random around the menage and the horse popped over when he least expects. On the principle that familiarity breeds contempt, the more cavalletti and low jumps that the rusher is popped over, the quieter he will become.

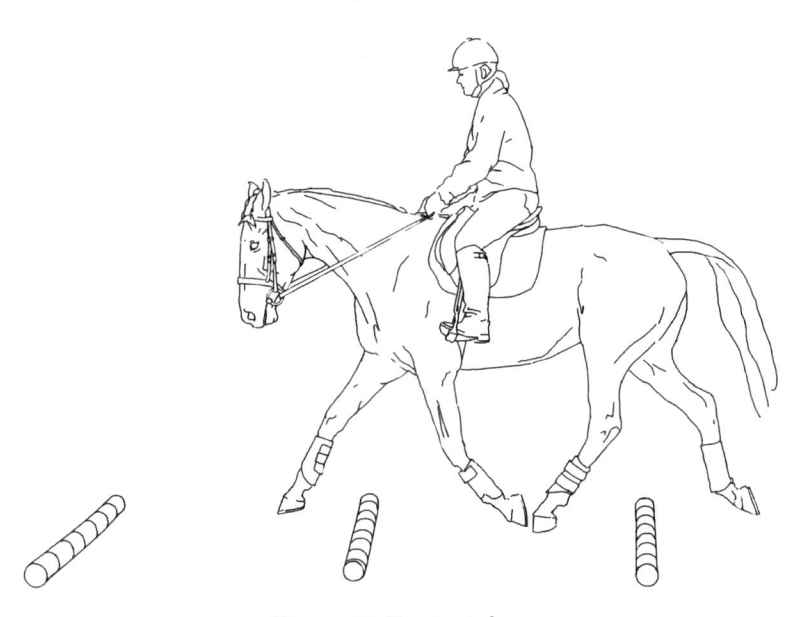

Figure 81 *Trotting poles*

Some people train their horses over trotting poles and cavaletti to such a degree that the horse begins to measure his take-off stride of his own volition. With a free-going horse the rider merely points the horse's head in the direction of the obstacle and it will jump it with a reasonable parabola. Advocates of this method sometimes take it to extremes, where in theory, if the distances are correct, a completely trained horse will take on a variety of single and combination fences.

With the best will in the world, the designer of showjumping or cross country courses cannot produce the correct distances for every horse in the competition. Therefore the author of these thoughts thinks it better that the rider assists the horse to arrive at the correct take-off point for a single fence and to stand back off a second and/or third part of a combination, rather than getting too close under the fence, thus causing a refusal, knock-down or fall.

Figure 82 a,b *The take-off stride.........*

Old fashioned hunting prints depict riders going over fences with the reins in one hand and hunting whip held aloft in the other. In practice the riders hit the horse with the whip on the take-off stride and referred to this as 'lifting' the horse over the fence. No man can lift over half a ton of horseflesh over a fence and what they did in fact do was to 'give the horse the office' to take-off at that particular stride.

Given some thought, it could be that the 'office' given on the take-off stride is too late and almost superfluous, as by then the horse should have made up its own mind whether to take on the obstacle or refuse. Old authors on the subject of riding to hounds suggested that the horse should be gathered or 'made up' (its mind made up for it) some twenty or thirty yards before the jump. This they probably did with whip and spur. The modern forward seat, which in its purity

94

should not vary on approach, take-off or landing, calls for a willing response to the aids on the part of the horse. Though the acute angle of the rider's foot and lower leg (the result of a deep heel) is the *sine qua non* that keeps the rider in the saddle, with this locked ankle joint it is difficult to give energetic driving aids.

If a horse starts to hesitate or refuse at an obstacle, it should be taken into an area devoid of jumps and schooled in elementary dressage until it responds to a mere vibration of the hard calf muscles, which are the result of a deep heel. The spur or schooling whip, applied to the horse's hollow side, will increase the severity of the leg aid when required.

Irrational use of whip and spur will never succeed in persuading an unwilling horse to jump. On the contrary, such methods make the horse violent, as very quickly it will anticipate that a thrashing will follow its refusal to jump. Consequently it will fight like a demon each time it is presented at an obstacle of which lack of experience makes it afraid.

The rider can only assist the horse to arrive at the take-off zone with its hocks under it and sufficient impetus to take the partnership over the fence. To this end the horse should be gathered between hand and leg some thirty yards from the jump.

Figure 82 c ....*and landing*

Working canter or even collected canter is the stride required. The rider looks at the take-off zone and then through acquired experience lengthens - not quickens - the last three strides before take-off. In modern parlance this is called 'seeing a stride'.

The take-off stride is calculated as being no nearer than one to one-and-a-half times the height of the jump as measured from its highest point (see figures 79c, 82b).

Refusals

When a young horse refuses to jump an obstacle, many riders punish the horse with whip and spur on the assumption it has been downright rebellious. On the contrary, it may be of a nervous disposition and either afraid of a strange jump or frightened of rapping itself. Alternatively it may be a really nappy horse, who, feeling its rider slightly hesitant with the driving and restraining aids, seizes the opportunity to run out or stop.

In all cases like these, no useful or long-term benefit can be gained by whipping or spurring the horse in an irrational way. It may get results on the first few refusals, but soon the horse will realise what comes next after a refusal and either nap violently or take the bit and rush its fences. Whilst a 'rusher' may take on and clear a reasonable single fence, it is almost impossible to get it right over the subsequent obstacles of a show jumping course. Even at cross country events one sees much sawing and yanking at the reins between fences.

Therefore it is logical to accept that the horse should be trained to approach the fences as calmly as it would trot down a country lane. Nine times out of ten refusals can be lessened, and in time eliminated, by merely lowering the fence at the first refusal rather then after dozens of abortive attempts.

As mentioned before, the refuser should be given a few minutes schooling on the flat with various movements in lateral work to get it listening to the leg aids. This is most important as when the horse lowers its neck on the last three strides before the fence, it is the rider's leg aids which stop the horse from ducking out left or right.

In the author's youth it was more common for horses in harness to jib than saddle horses to nap - there being more of the former. Jibbing is passive resistance: napping violent. It used to be advised that when a horse jibbed, its handler should recite 'The Wreck of the Hesperus' before doing anything. By the time the recitation was finished, the human being was less likely to resort to irrational punishment to resolve the problem.

Working on this premise, when the horse refuses to jump, the rider should stop and question whether interference or lack of assistance from the human half of the partnership was a contributory factor to the refusal. Whilst not quite going to the length of reciting some favourite poem, it would give a time lapse wherein the rider could think rationally, rather than adopting the 'up and at 'em' approach of the aggressive horseman.

d) Approaching the jump for the second time, the horse now going straight.

a) Horse inclined back across the line of approach.

b) Horse half-circled to the right.

c) Rudimentary turn on the forehand.

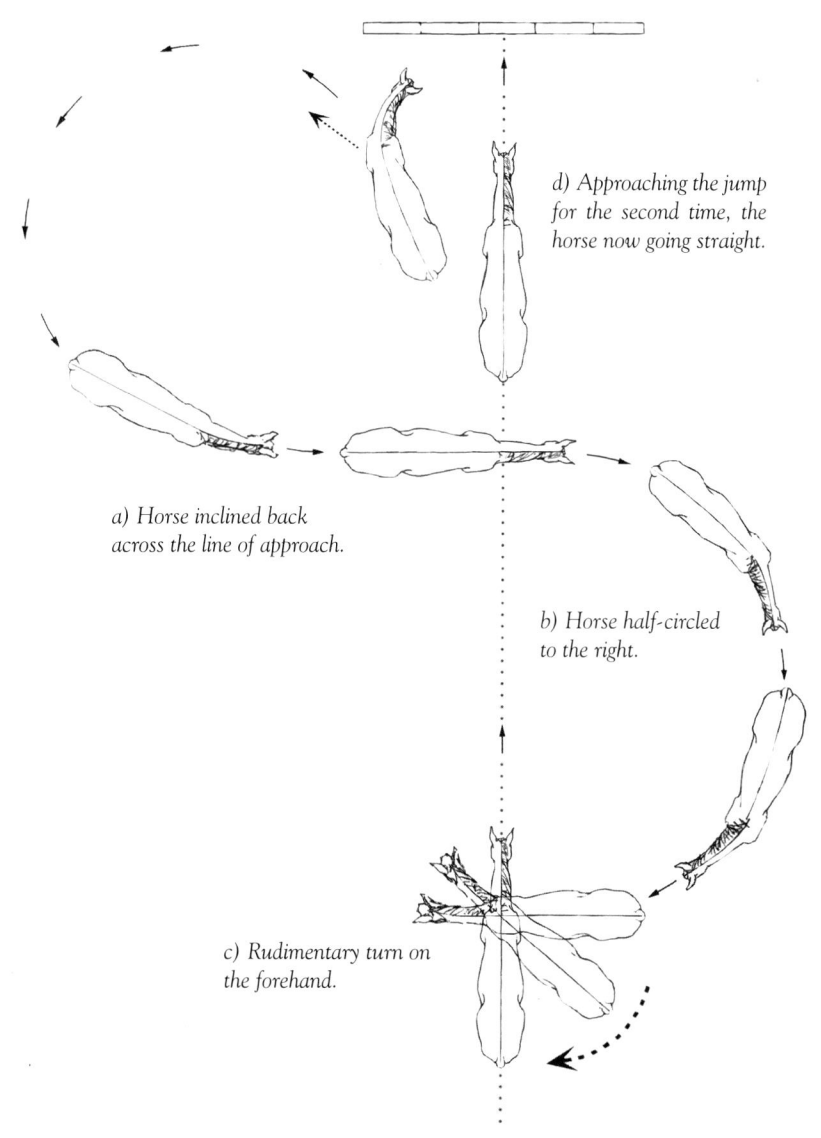

Figure 83 *Sorting out a run-out*

If the horse runs out or is turned to the left after a refusal, it should be inclined back across the line of approach to the jump (figure 83a), and then half-circled to the right (figure 83b). Finally, it should be brought back to track with an energetic right leg aid to produce a rudimentary turn on the forehand to the right (figure 83c).

Having disciplined the horse to pay more attention to this leg aid, all that is necessary is for that individual aid to be dominant on the approach to the take-off (figure 83d).

This manoeuvre would be treated as a technical second refusal in a competition and so is not viable. However, when at the competing stage, the refusal is probably a rider fault rather than nappiness or timidity on the part of the horse.

Loose Schooling over Jumps

At horse sales abroad, and more recently at those in this country, horses are lunged over obstacles prior to the auction. Some trainers also have an oval or circular jumping course on their premises, over which to drive young horses with the lunge whip. It is also said that in Ireland youngsters are, or were, led across country by a man carrying a bowl of feed. The horse is fed each time it follows the man over some natural obstacle.

Where the horse has a tendency to rush its fences when loose schooled, the long reining saddle can be used. The outside rein over the horse's back and behind the loop on the saddle gives the trainer almost as much control as if it were ridden. Strides can be seen and arriving at take-off zones practised. Side reins or grass reins should never be used when an horse is being asked to jump.

None-the-less, once confidence is established, work under the saddle must start again from basics as the weight of the rider alters the horse's equilibrium. Time must be also allowed for physical and muscular development.

Keeping a Horse Sound

When a horse is kept to showjump, event, or carry its rider to hounds, the trainer is on the horns of a dilemma as to how much jumping the horse should be subjected to. In theory, the more jumping practice it gets, the more confident it becomes.

Conversely, there is the risk of knocks, concussion to joints or tendon strain. It is now common practice for the horse to wear protective boots at all times, but these have their own disadvantages. If too large they can restrict the flexing of the knee and pastern joints, thus being a contributory cause of fences being knocked down with the forelegs.

Conformation also plays a part. The horse with upright pasterns that goes happily in the heavy going of the hunting field would concuss its joints if regularly subjected to the hard-baked surface of some summer showjumping venues. Alternately, a long, sloping pastern may give an armchair ride for hacking, but be conducive to strains of the tendons and suspensory ligaments when landing over reasonably large fences. Needless to say, correct shoeing plays a part in minimising the risk of lameness.

Most people whose horses compete in jumping competitions have the use of an all-weather surface to school on, and many winter events are held in indoor menages. It therefore comes as a shock to horses trained in these conditions to suddenly be subjected to the hard or deep going of natural grassland. Their muscles, tendons and ligaments are not acclimatised to these conditions. A certain amount of slow exercise (walking or trotting) should be done alternately on the roads and on fallowed fields such as recently harvested early potato ground.

As it is with race-horses, it is always a matter of 'horses for courses'. Either the owner only enters for competitions where the ground conditions are suitable for their horse, or they must buy a horse whose make and shape will adapt to the types of riding surface in their area.

Chapter Ten
Thoughts on Bitting

Xenophon advocates the horseman owns at least two bits. 'Let one of them be smooth with discs on it good-sized; the other with the discs heavy and not standing so high, but with the echini sharp, so that when he seizes it, he may drop it from dislike of its roughness. Then when he shall have received the smooth bit in its turn, he will like its smoothness and do everything on the smooth bit which he has been trained to do on the rough'.

The translator of Xenophon says echini means 'sea-urchin' and so the discs on the rough bit were scalloped like the edges of the sea urchin's shell. Archaeological finds of bits used about the era of Xenophon show that the so-called smooth bit had large discs which prevented the horse closing its mouth.

Whilst these barbaric mouthpieces have thankfully become obsolete, I am inclined to agree with Xenophon's principle of fettling (preparing) the young horse's mouth with a strong bit so that it will ultimately go kindly in a mild one. The proviso is that whatever bit is used, it should be thick enough to prevent damaging the bars of the mouth. Needless to say, they should not be so thick as to prevent the horse closing its mouth, as were Xenephon's.

One often sees young horses kept in a mild bit long after they have acquired the habit of evading it in one form or another. Starting lungeing or long reining without any bit at all, the trainer must quickly go through the whole range of snaffles from rubber via double and single-jointed snaffles to half-moon or straight-bar until they have found the bit to which the youngster is submissive. The correct bit is the one that persuades the horse to relax the lower jaw, allowing the impulsion created by the driving aids to be absorbed or go through according to the wishes of the trainer.

In mounted training, especially when hacking, a correctly fitted double bridle is not only less tiring to the rider but conforms to Xenophon's theory of strong and mild bits (figure 84). Any horse can be accustomed to the double bridle by walking it about on foot after the manner described in James Fillis' book 'Breaking and Riding'. Incidentally, whichever bit is used for schooling, the rider who is not confident or competent to ride in a double bridle should not be schooling a young horse.

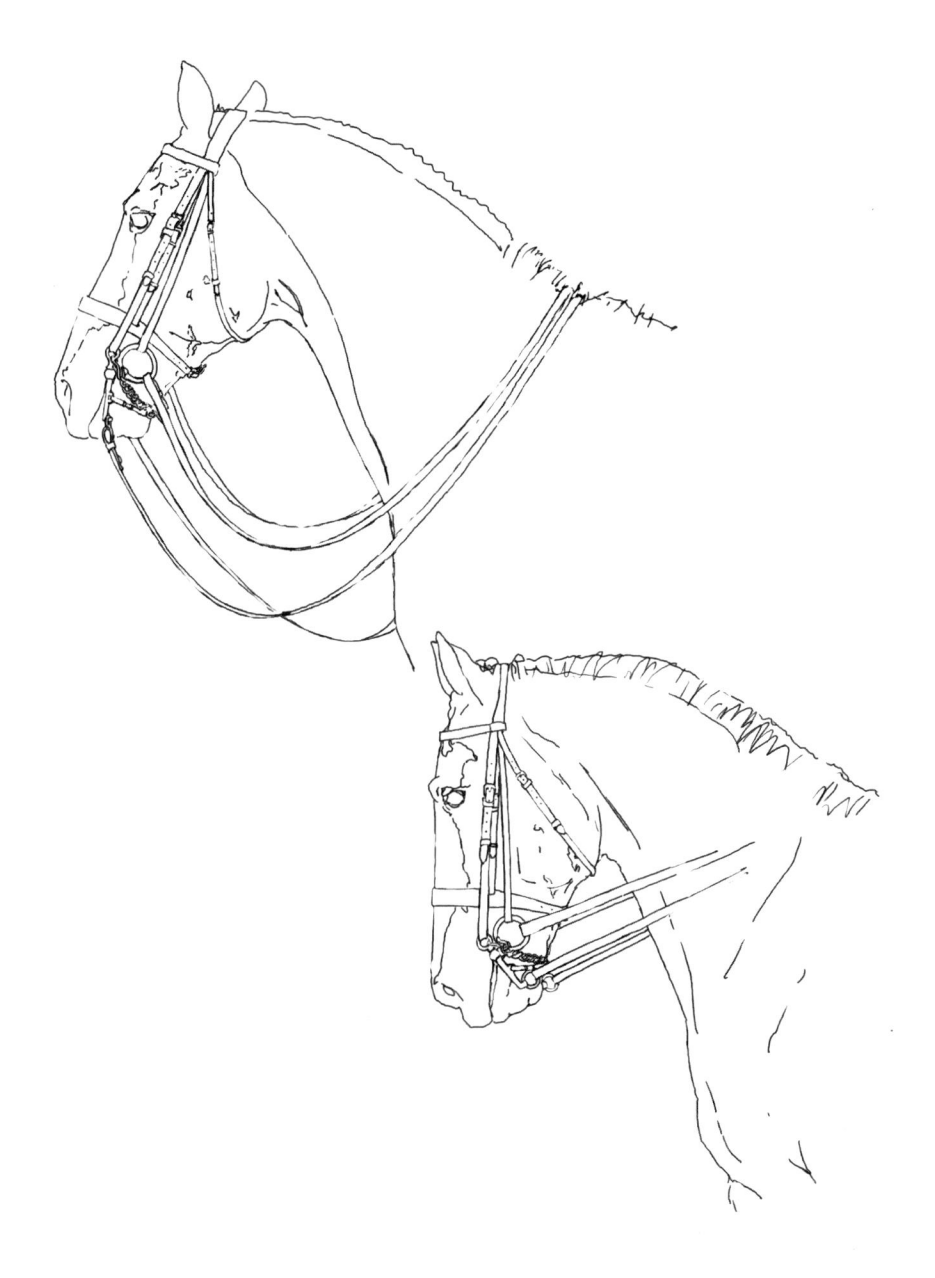

Figure 84 *Correctly fitted double bridle*

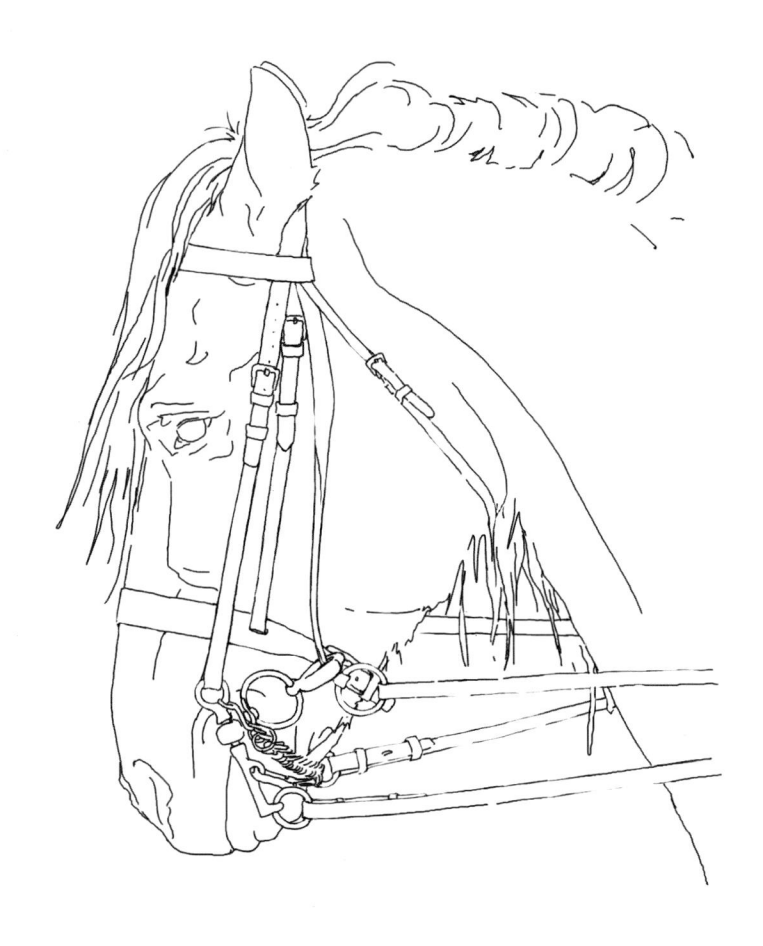

Figure 85 *Gag suitable for use with curb*

By alternating the use of the bridoon and the curb, the dedicated trainer will prevent their mount from establishing any of the numerous ploys to evade a correct contact with the bit. Where a spoilt horse leans heavily on the bridoon, a gag bit suitable for use in conjunction with a curb bit will usually get the desired result (figure 85).

When gags are employed by themselves, a standing martingale should be used to prevent the head being raised above the desired height (figure 86). (The curb rein of a double bridle has a more positive effect.)

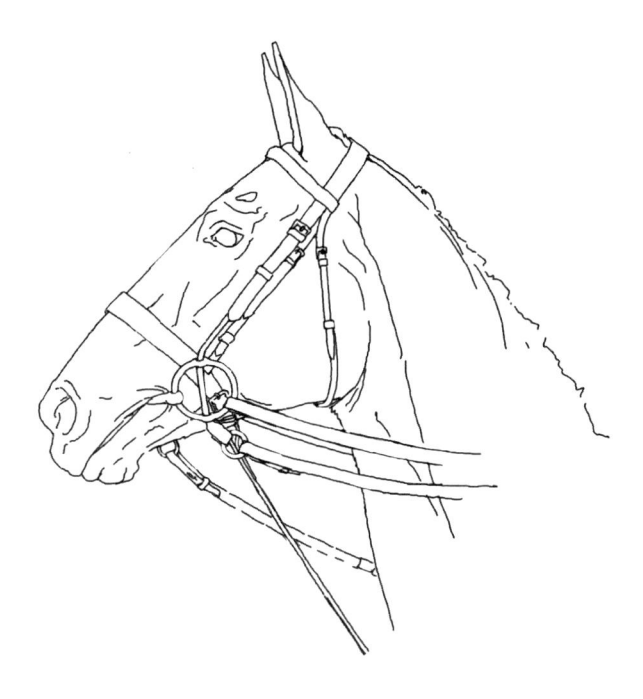

Figure 86 *Gag with extra rein to bit ring and standing martingale attached to cavesson noseband*

I consider Pelhams of any variety to be neither one thing nor the other. Those used with roundings to a single rein are an abomination. Even the Western rider, who ultimately requires his horse to go in a curb bit held in one hand, first schools his steed in the hackamore as well as the curb bit.

It is truly said that 'if there were a key (bit) for every horse's mouth, the loriners (bit makers) would be the best horsemen'. Therefore, whenever bit evasions occur, look first to the opposite ends of the reins to the horse's mouth for the cause of the problem.

Glossary

There are many terms in equitation for one and the same thing. Below are listed some of the terms used in this book and elsewhere which may cause confusion.

Balance / Horizontal Equilibrium / Outline / Ramener (French)
When the horse carries the rider and itself with the weight equally distributed on all four legs. This can only be achieved by patient schooling to develop the muscles to cope with the extra weight of the rider.

Direct Flexion / Longitudinal Bend / Acceptance of the Bit / A Good Mouth
Should be aimed for at the very beginning of training. Correctly done it absorbs any superfluous impulsion through an arched neck and a relaxed jaw.
See also 'collection'.

Faulty Flexion / Overbent / Over the Bit
Face behind the vertical, highest point of flexion half way down the neck, jaw clamped tight on the bit and majority of weight on the forehand (figure 56). See also 'above the bit'.

Lateral Flexion / Bend
Horse bent laterally through the whole of its body, hoof prints should fit exactly on the arc of the circle being ridden.

Faulty Lateral Flexion / Rubber Necking
Horse overbending laterally at the withers with lower jaw clamped tight; thus escaping contact and falling in or out of a circle (figures 43, 75), likewise veering to left or right when being ridden in straight lines.

Above the Bit / Star Gazing
As the first name implies: horse looking up at sky, bulge on the underline of the neck which causes the back to hollow, thereby restricting the hind legs from becoming engaged (figure 58).
N.B. In both above the bit and over the bit, the horse can lean on the hand (strong contact), pull away (rush off), or get behind the bit and refuse contact to the extent of napping.

Collection / Engagement / Submission / Rassembler (French)
Co-ordinated driving and restraining aids persuade the horse to shorten its stride and bring the hind legs more under its body (engagement). More weight is carried

on the hindquarters than in horizontal equilibrium. In a hypothetically perfect rassambler the horse would be in outline with a relaxed lower jaw, murmuring on the bit, obedient to minute aids and responsive at all times to its rider.

On the Forehand / Behind the Bit / Not Going Forward
The opposite to the above. A greater weight is carried on the forelegs than in horizontal equilibrium. Lower jaw clamped tight on the bit and horse stopping or turning to an individual rein aid. Hind legs trail behind and are thus unable to create impulsion (see figure 52). The head may be in front of or behind the vertical.

Horse Falling Out / Falling Out through the Shoulder / Shoulders Falling Out / Shoulder-In Position
All are ways of expressing the position shown in Chapter 8 figure 66. See Index for further examples.

Horse Falling In / Falling In through the Shoulder / Shoulders Falling In / Shoulder-Out Position
All are ways of expressing the position shown in Chapter 8 figure 68. See Index for further examples.

Soft side / Hollow side
The side to which the horse is naturally incurved. Even with extensive gymnastic training aimed to straighten the crooked horse, it will always tend to hollow the side to which it is naturally incuved in an effort to evade being collected. See also references in Index.

Stiff side
The opposite to the above.

Tyro
Novice or beginner.

Napping
The horse violently refuses to be ridden away from home, or in the direction its rider wants it to go.

Jibbing
Stubborn and passive resistance. The horse plants all four legs firmly on the ground and refuses to move.

Bibliography

Thinking Riding Books I and II	Molly Sivewright
The Art of Horsemanship	Xenophon (Translation M. H. Morgan)
Breaking and Riding	James Fillis (Translation M. H. Hayes)
Illustrated Horse Breaking	Capt. Horace Hayes
The Complete Training of Horse and Rider	Alois Podhajsky
Equitation	Henry Wynmalen
Dressage	Henry Wynmalen
School for Horse and Rider	Jack Hance
Academic Equitation	General Decarpentry
Understanding Equitation	Jean Saint-Fort Paillard
Reflections on the Equestrian Art	Nuno Olivera
Riding Reflections	P Santini

Index

above the bit	64, 67, 104
acceptance of the bit	104
balance	60, 64, 67, 104
beanstick	11-14
behind the bit	58-59, 60-61, 71-73, 105
bitting	7, 100-103
bitting (lungeing)	36, 37
breastplate	31, 32
bridoon	102
canter leads (on lunge)	40, 41
canter leads (under saddle)	79-82, 84-89
canter strike-off	57, 80-82, 84-87
cavalletti	92-93
cavesson	30-31
cavesson with bit straps	42, 43
cavesson with bridle and bit	37
changing the rein (on lunge)	39-40
collection	66, 104
Comanche bridle	24-25
contact	62-63
counter-canter	89, 92
crooked horse	70-73
crupper	31, 32
curb bit	7, 102
deep heel	63
diagonal aids	68-69, 72
direct flexion	63, 70, 104
double bridle	100-101
driving pad	48, 49
empathy	9
engagement	104
ewe neck	65
falling in (on lunge)	52-54, 105
falling in through shoulder (under saddle)	
in trot	83-84, 105
in canter	88-89, 105
falling out (on lunge)	51-54, 105

falling out through shoulder (under saddle)	
in trot	83, 105
in canter	86-87, 105
faulty flexion	104
faulty lateral flexion	104
Fillis, James	100, 106
foreleg, holding up a	26-27
free forward movement	58
gag bit	102-3
gait(s)	70
golden rule, the	68
good mouth	63, 104
grass reins	43, 49, 98
hackamore	103
half-halt	70-72
half-pass	77, 79
halter	11-14
hollow side	105
horizontal equilibrium	60, 104
inside out	80
jaw, relaxation of the lower	63
jaws, crossing the	63
jibbing	96, 105
lateral aids	62, 68, 69, 72
lateral movements	74-79
lead rope, holding	20
leg aids	58-62, 89, 95
leg-yield	75
long rein walk	60-61
long reining saddle	48, 49
loose schooling over jumps	98
manger block	23
napping (on lunge)	55, 105
napping (under saddle)	59, 86, 97, 105
not going forward	105
on the forehand	105
one-sided horse	70-73

107

one-sided horse/mouth (under saddle in canter)	80-82, 86-89
one-sided horse/mouth (under saddle in trot)	82-84
open rein	59
outline	55, 64-65, 104
overbending	64, 66, 104
parabola	92
pelham bit	103
ramener	67, 104
rassembler	64, 104
rearing	31, 32, 33, 47, 86
refusals	96-98
rein aids	59-62
rein back, teaching	33
reining back (under saddle)	69
renvers	76-77
rhythm	70
rubbernecking	52, 85, 104
running back (on the lunge)	35-36, 46
running back (under saddle)	62-63
running off (on the lunge)	34, 35
rushing fences	96
schooling to the aids	58-62
schooling whip	63
self-carriage	66
shoulder-in	51-54, 76-77, 105
shoulder-out	52-53, 77, 105
side-stepping	56-57
soft side	37-39, 45 105
soundness	98-99
spurs	7, 63
standing martingale	102
stargazing	64, 67, 104
side reins	31, 35, 38-39, 42-47, 98
stiff side	37-9, 45 105
straightening the crooked horse	72-73
submission	63, 65-66, 104
suppleness	5, 28, 56, 78-79, 82, 86, 86
tact, equestrian; see empathy	69, 89
tempo	70
travers	77-8
trot (ting) poles	92-93
turn on the forehand (under saddle)	62, 68, 72-73, 74, 97
turn on the forehand (teaching)	34
turn on the haunches	72, 75
tying a plough rope	50
tyro	105
Xenophon	7, 100, 106